"Natasha Daniels' memoir *Ou*… …es her social anxiety journey with psychoeducation and invaluable tools. Full of hope and healing, *Out of My Shell* is a must-read for individuals with social anxiety, loved ones and providers wanting to better understand the nuances of this disorder."

—**Amanda Petrik-Gardner,** LCPC, LPC, LIMHP, @anxietyocdtreatment and author of *The Compulsive Reassurance Seeking Workbook*

* * *

"*Out of My Shell* is a painful yet beautifully inspirational memoir. A lifetime of quiet torment and suffering, filled with social anxiety and self-doubt, is met with vulnerability, grace and perseverance. Natasha Daniels is the epitome of bravery and self-compassion, witnessed firsthand with her toughest and most important therapy client of all, her younger self."

—**Josh Spitalnick,** Ph.D., ABPP, CEO/owner of Anxiety Specialists of Atlanta, co-author of *The Complete Guide to Overcoming Health Anxiety*

* * *

"With truth, kindness and compassion, Natasha Daniels shares what healing from social anxiety can look like in a real life. In *Out of My Shell*, her lyrical writing brings the reader close, and her ultimate self-acceptance helps to heal the reader along the way. Don't miss this gorgeous memoir."

—**Rachael Herron,** bestselling memoirist

* * *

"*Out of My Shell* is a profound and transformative exploration of the journey from social anxiety to self-acceptance. Her vivid storytelling captures the raw emotions associated with growing up feeling different in a way that is both deeply personal and universally relatable."

—**Kimberley Quinlan,** author of *The Self-Compassion Workbook for OCD*

"In this unflinching memoir, Natasha Daniels lays bare her agonizing struggle with crippling social anxiety. Her intimate narrative charts a powerful metamorphosis from a lifetime of inner turmoil to hard-won self-acceptance. Fusing poignant storytelling with invaluable psychological insights, this book inspires courage to shed one's protective shell. An uplifting read for anyone longing to blossom into their most authentic, luminous self."

—**Amanda Stern,** author of *Little Panic: Dispatches from an Anxious Life*

"Natasha Daniels' memoir is a deeply personal, refreshingly honest and truly authentic story that will inspire every person struggling with fears, worries and anxieties about social performance to find their path to being loved, seen and heard. A must-read!"

—**Patricia E. Zurita Ona,** Psy.D., author of *Escaping the Emotional Rollercoaster, Acceptance and Commitment Skills for Perfectionism and High-Achieving Behaviors* and *Living Beyond OCD*

OUT OF MY SHELL

also by this author

How to Parent Your Anxious Toddler
Natasha Daniels
ISBN 978 1 84905 738 7
eISBN 978 1 78450 148 8

The Grief Rock
A Book to Understand Grief and Love
Natasha Daniels
Illustrated by Lily Fossett
ISBN 978 1 83997 439 7
eISBN 978 1 83997 440 3

Crushing OCD Workbook for Kids
50 Fun Activities to Overcome OCD with CBT and Exposures
Natasha Daniels
Illustrated by Richy K. Chandler
ISBN 978 1 83997 888 3
eISBN 978 1 83997 889 0

of related interest

Things I Got Wrong So You Don't Have To
48 Lessons to Banish Burnout and Avoid Anxiety
for Those Who Put Others First
Pooky Knightsmith
ISBN 978 1 83997 267 6
eISBN 978 1 83997 268 3

The Ultimate Anxiety Toolkit
25 Tools to Worry Less, Relax More, and Boost Your Self-Esteem
Risa Williams
Illustrated by Jennifer Whitney and Amanda Way
ISBN 978 1 78775 770 7
eISBN 978 1 78775 771 4
Ultimate Toolkits for Psychological Wellbeing Series

OUT OF MY SHELL

Overcoming Social Anxiety from Childhood to Adulthood

Natasha Daniels

Jessica Kingsley Publishers
London and Philadelphia

First published in Great Britain in 2025 by Jessica Kingsley Publishers
An imprint of John Murray Press

1

Content Warning: *This book mentions anxiety, bullying, death, loss of a loved one, medical conditions and situations, suicidal ideation, violence and gunshots.*

A CIP catalogue record for this title is available from the British Library and the Library of Congress

ISBN 978 1 80501 197 2
eISBN 978 1 80501 198 9

Printed and bound in the United States by Integrated Books International

Jessica Kingsley Publishers' policy is to use papers that are natural, renewable and recyclable products and made from wood grown in sustainable forests. The logging and manufacturing processes are expected to conform to the environmental regulations of the country of origin.

Jessica Kingsley Publishers
Carmelite House
50 Victoria Embankment
London EC4Y 0DZ

www.jkp.com

John Murray Press
Part of Hodder & Stoughton Ltd
An Hachette Company

To my three children, Chloe, Xander and Alex, who have found creative ways to make my social anxiety squirm.
I love living a life of adventure with you all.

To Jimmie, who showed me how to laugh at the seriousness of life.
Your warmth will always be a source of comfort, now and forever.

Chapter 1
Now

I pulled the covers up tight to protect me from my ever-growing insecurities. The room was dark and quiet, but my mind was spinning. *Everyone hates me. I'm an outsider. I can't stomach this anymore.*

I curled up into a fetal position and hugged my knees. Do I really need to get up today? I wondered if I could just hit the pause button, freeze life while I tried to catch my breath. I didn't need any new information for my brain to process. I didn't want any new experiences. I just wanted to get lost in the darkness where life simply didn't exist.

My head was throbbing. How long had I been lying here? I felt too vulnerable for the harshness of the world. I felt too fragile to take another hit. I just wanted to hide forever. The world felt unsafe. As if it was a packed audience waiting to see me stammer on my lines, waiting to mock my efforts.

I hadn't felt this way in such a long time. I had almost convinced myself that my social anxiety was gone, off to torment another soul. What had happened? Why did I crumble like a day-old cookie the minute my social anxiety was triggered? Why had I once again given my power away?

Voices from the other room shattered my silence. I heard laughing that quickly turned into arguing. It seemed as if that was how it went these days with my two youngest.

"Give it to me!" Alex demanded, her voice booming from her tiny frame. She reminded me of myself at that age, petite with a feisty personality.

"No! It's mine!" taunted Xander. He stood barely an inch taller than her.

"I'm telling Mom!" Alex threatened, a hint of giddiness in her tone.

"Shhhh," my husband said. "Your mom is sleeping."

I rolled over and felt a thickness in my throat. I should have been out there instead of in here licking my wounds—wounds that were so trivial they didn't even deserve to be licked.

Get up, Natasha! Time to get your big girl pants on and shake this off. I rolled out of bed. My body ached as I pulled the covers off. My eyes felt as if two heavy sacks of sand were weighing them down. I felt disoriented as I stumbled to the closet. *Shake it off.*

Was this how my dad felt?

My body stiffened as images of my dad lying in a dark room danced behind my eyes. Flashbacks of my childhood started to whirl around me. Darkened rooms. Psychiatric units. Hushed tones. Police. Another suicide attempt. Another visit to another unit.

I gulped hard.

No, you are not your dad! I went into the darkened closet to grab some fresh clothes. *My kids don't deserve a childhood like mine. Especially over something as stupid as this.*

Where had all my progress gone? A wave of nausea overcame me. I thought I had come so far. Now look at me. My face warmed as I thought about what had caused this backslide. It was so stupid. I couldn't talk to anyone about this, not even my husband. He would just tell me not to care what other people thought. It seemed so easy for him.

Jimmie was the stoic type. He was a tree with deep roots that stood firm in even the most ferocious storm. He wasn't the emotional type. He was a protector, a provider and as dependable as a flashlight in a storm, but he wasn't big into feelings. He gave me my space. He knew something was off, but he was not one to voluntarily rock a boat.

From deep within my fog, I heard a faint knock at the door. Jimmie popped his head in, not fully committing to entering my new world. In my mind's eye, I could feel him just standing there, trying to make sense of the metamorphosis that stole his wife seemingly overnight.

"Are you mad at me?" he finally whispered, the first hint of an acknowledgment that something was not right. I peered out from under my blanket. I could see his frame in the door, his broad shoulders and square jaw silhouetted by the light behind him.

"No," I mumbled from beneath the layer of protection, too embarrassed to elaborate. "I'm fine," I lied, hoping that would suffice.

I had spent most of the day in bed, highly unusual for a person like me who greeted the sun and tucked in the moon.

I just couldn't do it today, I just couldn't.

But I had a visceral response to lying in a dark room in the middle of the day. It opened old childhood wounds and made me feel sick to my stomach.

I grabbed a T-shirt and some jeans. The denim felt scratchy and uncomfortable against my skin as I forced my legs through. *You're doing this. Go out there and be a mom. Stop feeling bad for yourself. Enough already.*

I hadn't heard that internal voice in a while. The one that mocked me, berated me, whispered and told me all my faults. The one that I had named "Paro" for paranoid, when I had finally decided to fight my social anxiety and the steady diet of social paranoia he fed me.

I knew how to beat anxiety. In fact, I spent most of my life studying the enemy up close and personal. And when that wasn't enough I went to graduate school to formally get a degree in it. Yes, anxiety and I go way back.

Somewhere between my father's suicide attempts, my sister's intensive treatment centers, and the thousands of therapy sessions I was dragged to, I decided to be a therapist. Ironically, none of those therapy sessions were ever for me. I was the poster child for middle children. The peacemaker. The one to steady an ever-rocking boat. Never one to draw any attention to myself. My family had enough issues, they didn't need to deal with mine.

After one of my father's suicide attempts, I decided to take matters in my own hands. "I'm going to be a therapist," I remember telling my mom. "No one is helping him. How can someone be so sick for so long?"

She just shrugged, looking tired and defeated.

I never became a pioneer in bipolar treatment. I never saved the world, and I never saved my dad for that matter. But in the silent suffering of my childhood, I developed a deep understanding for other children like me. I understood the anxious child, the one who didn't rock the boat. The one who lay in bed with her sheets up to her neck, waiting for bad guys to attack. The one who threw up when nervous and replayed every conversation in her head.

Chapter 2
Then

Washington Avenue

We were a chaotic family of six. My sister Leigh was the oldest, followed by Jake, me and Allison.

We didn't have much structure in our lives, but on Fridays we always had dinner at my grandparents' house. We all piled into the station wagon to make the quick trek to the large house with big white pillars in the town next to ours. My mom's parents were her anchor. They had steadied her wobbles her entire life. They were our anchor too. They had rescued her often, which in turn rescued us. They had bought our house, provided ongoing financial support, and poured the glue that kept our cracked family together. It wasn't until the glue stopped pouring that I realized how broken we really were. I think my mom eventually had that epiphany too.

Their house was warm and inviting. The smell of chicken soup and parsley permeated the air. The backyard was a sea of green to play in.

"Tashala," Nana said as she gave my small six-year-old frame a tight hug, squeezing my ribs together. My nostrils filled with the smell of parsnip and cigarettes. Her white cotton candy hair covered most of my nose, making it hard to breathe. I waited for her to release her grip. It didn't take long.

She quickly let go and said, "Joel is in the living room, go say hi," her gaze already moving on to focus on my mom.

Joel was my cousin. Really my only cousin. My dad came to America alone and we never saw his side of the family. A lost soul in a lost land. My mom, on the other hand, was not nearly as mysterious. She had one sister and that sister had one son. Joel lived in Brooklyn, and we only saw him a few times a month.

I smiled at Joel and tried to give him my best happy face. "Hi!" I said, falling a bit flat. He barely looked up, his disheveled hair framing his freckled face, his eyes remaining focused on the TV. Joel was typically underwhelmed by my existence. I had wracked my brain trying to understand why. Joel was my age; in fact, we were born only two months apart. You would think it would be a friendship made in utero. But Joel never paid me much attention.

My brother Jake came into the living room, took a scoop of candies from a bowl and discreetly poured them into his pocket. "Hey," he said as he nodded to my cousin.

Joel bounced off the couch. "Hey, Jake!" he said, his monochrome tone turning multicolored with enthusiasm. My stomach churned with the contrast of the syrupy sweet greeting he received. I was tired of being second fiddle. I opened my mouth to say something, but they were both heading for the door.

My older sister Leigh didn't even try to compete. Maybe she was the smart one. She sat in between my aunt and Nana on the couch. She soaked up the spitfire questions being thrown at her, glowing in the attention she received.

I wished I could be like that. I wished I could just dismiss my brother and cousin and find my own place. A place that felt like home; a place that felt like belonging. But that type of peace wouldn't be found for decades to come—if ever.

I dashed out of the room, convinced I might be missing some secret handshake or private game. I ran through the house in a controlled frenzy, trying to find where Jake and Joel had gone. I slid across the heavy glass doors and headed outside to the backyard. I heard laughing in the distance and followed the sound.

"What are you guys doing?" I said, trying to catch my breath. Neither of them looked up, focused on something they had found on the ground. "Can I play?" I asked, a hint of desperation in my voice. They both shrugged. That was the closest to a "yes" I was going to get, so I stayed, forcing the twosome to become a threesome.

At the time, I thought those Friday night dinners were a staple, just like our bright-yellow house and the neighborhood crew. We were firmly anchored, our roots healthy, deep and alive. I look back and think our small world was almost picture perfect, at least to my six-year-old eyes.

* * *

"Here, I got these for you," Mom reached into a garbage bag of loot from a garage sale.

I held up the jean shorts against my small body. "Thanks!" I said, tracing the small satiny patch on the pocket. "What's this?"

She looked up from the bag and her face broke into an

awkward smile. It made my stomach flutter in a way I didn't like. Later in life I would realize it was her uncomfortable smile, a warning that bad news was coming.

"That's the shape of Texas," she said with a forced laugh. "We are moving there soon." She dug her head back in for more clothes as I stood staring at her. "And I got this for you!" she said, handing Leigh a shirt.

I swallowed hard, my head starting to feel disconnected from my body. I didn't understand what she meant. Most of my mom's news would be delivered like a grenade. Pull the pin, drop, and run for cover. This was just the first explosion, there would be more to come.

My sisters and I crammed into the tiny pink room we shared. Leigh had her head under the pillow, and I could hear muffled sniffles. She had been like that for hours.

I sighed and walked into my brother's room. He was sitting on his bottom bunk. He had large exposed wooden beams on his ceiling, and I liked to hang on the rafters.

"It will be fine," he said, trying to comfort me. "We'll make new friends."

I thought about the friends I had, the only friends I had ever known. My eyes started to tear up.

"You can hang out here if you want," he said, noticing me struggle. I tried to blink away my tears and nodded okay. I let go of the rafters and fell onto his top bunk. I lay there for a while, listening to my sister sob, wondering what she knew that we didn't.

Chapter 3
Now

I sat in the big, oversized chair in my office waiting for my first session to arrive. I rolled my neck back and forth. I always felt better in my office.

I picked up a squish ball and bounced it back and forth nervously in my hands. I didn't like the way I was feeling. It scared me and brought me back to dark days that were not my own, days I would rather forget.

I had seven clients today. I took a deep breath and reminded myself that I could do this, I always do. I never let myself down and, more importantly, I never let anyone else down. I stared at the clock. Tick. Tick. Tick. Ten minutes to go. The ticking sounds taunted me.

I had learned from a very young age to box away bad feelings and not show any cracks. I was good at shutting things down, turning them off, putting them away for another time. It was a big part of my survival as a child and the dysfunctional skill had withstood the test of time.

I startled when I heard the ding dong from my office's front door sensor announcing that my 2 p.m. session had arrived. I inhaled deeply to reset my body and mind.

* * *

That night I tossed and turned and could not sleep. My body ached for rest, but my mind had other ideas. I thought about a few of the sessions I had had that day. I thought about the seven-year-old girl with an intense fear of dogs and the 13-year-old girl who was immobilized by the fear of rejection. I was her twin at that age, struggling with the same feelings. I imagined that my 13-year-old self would've loved to hang out with her, our insecurities cocooning each other. It was easy to help her—like riding an old bike; her issues felt familiar and the words she needed to hear fell effortlessly from my mouth.

My therapy practice was very specialized. I only worked with children and teens who had anxiety or obsessive compulsive disorder (OCD). It was something I knew like the back of my hand, and I had almost a sixth sense on how to help.

Work was always refueling, even when I felt as if a dark cloud was trying to block out the sun's rays. To help others was healing to myself. But the darkness was back, and sleep felt like a long-term goal I was probably not going to achieve. What would life be like if I'd had therapy as a child? Would *my* social anxiety have improved or been blissfully silenced? Would it have saved me years of feeling alone and rejected in a room full of people?

I hoped I was saving kids the pain I couldn't prevent for myself. Anxiety can destroy you from the inside out. It can taunt you. It can become a lifelong partner in a journey you didn't sign up for, riding shotgun, narrating every ugly observation and mishap in gruesome detail.

I was surrounded by therapy as a child. I participated in my father's sessions. I was forced to sit in many uncomfortable plastic chairs in stark white rooms, where we had to be buzzed in and out. I had visited old houses with old therapists, trying to breathe new life into their building and their practice. I had sat on many couches, talked about many things, but not once was it about me.

I imagined what it would be like if my six-year-old self came to see me. What would I say to her? Could I help her? Could I save her from the quiet years of torment and suffering in which she firmly blamed herself? Social anxiety loves to do that. It loves to hide behind the curtain, quietly whispering observations to tear you down.

Sometimes in sessions with older teens I would have them go back in time and talk to their younger selves. Social anxiety is cruel. Its words can slice through even the toughest exterior. "Would you talk to your five-year-old self that way?" I would ask. "Say what you just said about yourself but tell it to the five-year-old you." If they had a picture of their younger self, that was even better.

It can be a powerful exercise, even for a teenager. It can make them hear the voice for what it truly is: social anxiety, the hidden tapeworm that is nourished by self-hate and self-doubt.

How would my six-year-old self feel about me now? Sitting here, wallowing in pain, giving my power away once again. *She* deserved better than this.

I toyed with an idea that was trying to take shape in my head. I stewed on it, tasted the flavor of possible change. I had worked hard on my social anxiety. So hard for these past few years that I naively hung a huge banner in my mind's eye announcing victory. *Paro no longer lives here,* it read. *The parasite is gone!* That is, until he returned with a vengeance, mocking my victory, ripping the banner and taking his seat back at the helm.

Anxiety isn't something you get rid of, it's something you manage. It is something you shrink so tiny you don't have to stare at its ugly face. But I took my eyes off the ball. I let Paro slither back into the warmth of my insecurities, feeding on my doubts, and he tripled his size as he ate his way through my self-worth.

I needed to go way back. I needed to do the healing that I hadn't done before. Healing that could have prevented this new growth of insecurity from taking hold yet again.

I needed to help my younger selves, offer what I offer to everyone else. I needed to invite them in, one by one. Sit with them. Talk with them. Tell them what they needed to hear. Tell them what no one else ever did.

In my mind's eye, I heard the ding dong notifying me that someone was out in the hall. I got up from my big, cozy seat and wiped my clammy hands on my pants.

I saw her down the hall, her feet dangling from the seat. She had shoulder-length brown hair and a big gap where her front teeth used to be. She wore a satin burgundy jumpsuit with a yellow star on it. I remembered that outfit, it was glued to my skin when I was six.

She smiled nervously at me. I smiled back, trying to calm

her nerves. "Are you ready?" I asked. She nodded as I took her little hand in mine. "This is long overdue," I said. "I'm so sorry."

I took a deep breath and thought about what I wanted to say. My six-year-old self sat in an oversized chair staring back at me, her small body getting lost in the cushions. Miss Six looked around my office with big eyes. "What's this?" she asked, holding up my magnet balls.

"It's a fun fidget toy," I explained.

Her eyes narrowed and her tongue stuck out of her mouth, as she focused on pulling each tiny ball apart.

I let her play with the toy for a bit. I didn't know where to start. I mentally tripped over my words before they made it out of my mouth. She looked up, perhaps confused by my silence.

"So, how's life over on Washington Avenue these days?" I asked, squirming a bit in my seat. This session was harder than I thought it would be. I tried to center myself. *What is the purpose of this? What am I trying to accomplish?*

Luckily, once Miss Six warmed up she was a talker. She hummed to herself as she pulled the magnets apart and separated them by color, something I often did as well. She looked up and smiled. "Do you know where Texas is? We are moving there soon. I'm not sure what that will be like."

I unfortunately did. It wouldn't be easy. Her safe little world was about to land on its head.

She spoke rapidly, her eyes dancing around the room. She was more confident than I remembered. When did the layers of insecurities pile on, dulling this sparkly girl? I barely recognized her.

"My mom said I can walk to the A & P grocery store all by

myself when I'm seven. I really hope we don't move before then. I've been waiting my whole life to go there by myself. My brother and sister get to go there all by themselves and buy drinks, but I can't. I'm going to ride my bike there as soon as I'm allowed!"

I stared at my feet. *No,* I thought. *The A & P will burn down before then and you'll be gone before they rebuild it.* But I kept those details to myself.

"I have a few things I wanted to let you know," I said.

"Okay," she said, grasping my serious tone.

"There is going to be a lot of change for you," I started.

She nodded, putting more green balls in the pile. "I know," she said in an upbeat tone and started to hum again.

"Maybe even more than you know," I warned. "And you might doubt yourself. You might start to feel that you aren't important or lovable, or even likable. But I want you to remember how you feel right now. This is who you are supposed to be."

She stopped putting the green balls in a pile and looked up. Her mouth was open, but nothing was coming out. I looked down at my hands, paused and continued. "You notice things. You notice when people are upset. You notice when they are uncomfortable. You are very good at noticing these things. Not everyone can do that. But because of that you'll also notice small things that other people wouldn't. Like when someone doesn't like what you say or when someone doesn't want to play with you. You'll notice when people are angry or upset, even when other people don't like you. You are sensitive that way."

She nodded, as if her little ears could process my big words. "Like when Jake and Joel don't want me around? Or when I can tell that the boys in the neighborhood find my brother more fun than me?"

"Exactly," I said. "You can spend a lot of wasted years trying to get someone to like you, when you could be using that time to like yourself." I knew that was way over her six-year-old head, but I continued. "Your brother and cousin will always prefer to hang out with each other. That won't stop. But that doesn't mean there is something wrong with you. You just won't be everyone's first choice, and that's okay. The boys in the neighborhood prefer the cool older brother. That is actually pretty normal, that doesn't mean you're not fun or cool. As you have more experiences like those, your mind is going to make up some stories, stories about how you are not likable; stories about how no one wants to hang out with you, not even your family." I paused and looked to see if she was soaking in what I was saying.

She sat there, the magnets abandoned, the colored piles incomplete. Her eyes met mine. Yes, she was hanging on my every word.

I took a breath. "When you feel these things, you want to protect yourself. So, you look for more and more proof that people don't like you, that you are not likable. That way you can try and avoid the hurt that comes with it. But, if you look for proof, you'll always find it. Especially when someone is as observant as you. You can spend your whole life looking for this proof and when you find it, which you always will, it will shut you down, make you not trust the world or the people in it."

I knew I had lost her. I had talked way over her head. Her little eyes stared back at me, a blank expression on her face.

Even though I knew she wasn't following what I was saying, I couldn't help but continue. "That voice of doubt and rejection will be loud," I warned. "It will grow louder each year. But don't be afraid to question it. Learn to doubt the assumptions it brings. Not everything is black and white. Look for the gray."

I reached for a fidget toy and started to fiddle with it. "Anyway," I added, trying to sound more upbeat, "I just want you to know that how others see you doesn't define you. Okay?"

She shrugged her shoulders and quietly murmured, "Okay."

I paused and took a breath. There was not much else to say to Miss Six. I couldn't warn her about the many moves she would have or the frailty of her family's stability. I couldn't tell her that her dad's first suicide attempt would be only a few years away. I couldn't tell her that those seeds of rejection she was feeling would blossom into an overgrown garden of insecurities watered by every judgment or criticism that came her way. No, she'd have to figure out all that on her own.

Our time together was wrapping up. I helped her off the big chair and grabbed her pale little hand. I opened my office door and watched her walk out of the room. Her little hands swung back and forth as she moved down the hall. I had a sudden primal urge to run after her, wrap her in armor and hide her away. But that's not how life works. That's not how any of this works. I told myself, *She'll be okay. She always is*, as a sprinkle of doubt crept into my mind.

Chapter 4
Then

Hammerwood Avenue

"I think that's it, we're ready to go," my dad said as he put the last box into the U-Haul trailer. I sat on the top stoop watching. *How can that small trailer hold everything we own?*

I said goodbye to the bright-yellow house, with its cheerful smile. I took one last look as we pulled away from the house. Yellow paint was peeling on the windows, and you could see exposed raw wood in some places. Maybe the bright-yellow house wasn't as cheerful as I had thought.

The U-Haul drove away, and with that the first chapter in my life closed.

The drive from New Jersey to Texas was tedious, all of us crammed in like sardines for a trip that brought no happy endings.

I often fantasized what life would have looked like if we hadn't taken that trip away from stability. Would my confidence have continued to soar, the genetic seed of social anxiety left dormant, never to sprout?

But I would never get the opportunity to find out. The

genetic predisposition for anxiety was rooted deep within me and those seeds were about to get well watered.

* * *

My parents had no plans, not one. Not where my dad would work, not where we would live, not where we would even go to school. Nothing had been mapped out. Nothing had been carefully considered. We were nomads, all packed with no destination to end our journey.

Eventually we found an apartment. We piled out of the car, and I stood there staring at a sign that read "Apple Apartments."

"It's home," my mom said half to herself. A shiver ran down my spine. It didn't feel like home.

The apartment complex was uncharted territory for me and my siblings. We were used to the same actors, reading off the same lines, playing by all the same rules. Now we were off script with no lines or rules to follow. For a few months we became the neighborhood targets. The neighborhood kids made sure to let me know I was not welcome on their "turf." Leigh became the latest entertainment for some mean girls. I no longer felt safe roaming a neighborhood alone.

Eventually, my parents found a nice house in a quiet neighborhood on Hammerwood Avenue. It was in the middle of nowhere, but it brought back some security we desperately needed.

My dad decided to start his own dental lab. We all started to make friends and things felt more settled. We tentatively stepped on freshly poured stability.

I was placed in a large elementary school that seemed overcrowded and underfunded. The entire third grade was in one large open space, each class separated by flimsy room dividers. I sat on the floor trying hard to hear my teacher, being overwhelmed with all the noise and chaos around me. All the change was too much for my anxious mind and body.

* * *

Luckily, the next school year my parents found a small private school where they had real classrooms. It was exactly what we all needed. My parents had been able to finagle a full scholarship for all four of us and with that they had negotiated our stability.

All of us made friends. Allison was in kindergarten, I was in fourth grade, Jake was in sixth grade, and Leigh was in eighth grade. It was perfect, we were all finally at the same school. It felt nice to know I was not alone.

My personality bloomed again, after being wilted for a time. I flourished in the small environment and quickly found my voice and confidence. I made lots of friends and my days were filled with playdates and sleepovers. Jake, Leigh and Allison were doing the same.

My father's dental lab continued to grow. He had hired several employees and my mom spent her days managing their ever-growing business.

Life had started to stabilize.

Chapter 5
Now

I lived in a monochrome world, a two-dimensional existence. Everything seemed flat, everything tasted flat. I was getting concerned. This wasn't like me. It took all my energy to get the basics done and I just couldn't shake off this fog that was consuming me from the inside out.

I walked into the kitchen. Xander was curled up in a ball in our big bean bag, his big toe peeking out, his dark curly hair hanging over the other side. He was nine, but his small frame made him look much younger.

My youngest daughter, Alex, was sitting at the breakfast bar, her headphones on as she stared at her iPad, her feet moving to the music.

"Where's Chloe?"

She slurped her cereal, looked up, and was startled by my presence. "Oh, she's sleeping," she said, looking back at her iPad, spilling another spoonful of Cheerios into her mouth.

My oldest had started to hibernate in her bat cave most of the time, playing video games virtually with her friends. I would periodically get worried, but then I would remind myself that she was a teen and that's what teens do. She had struggled with so much social anxiety in elementary school that just hearing her laugh from inside her room made me feel good.

Mental illness is a funny thing. It doesn't isolate. It climbs a family tree like growing moss, making sure to cover each branch. Many people don't realize that anxiety and OCD are highly genetic. That they can dominate a generation, just like diabetes or heart disease can do.

Anxiety and OCD didn't skip a generation in my family. They didn't take time out to catch their breath. They dutifully grew, planting the next seeds and waiting for their next opportunity to grow.

But this time I was waiting, anticipating their arrival, protecting my side of the branch.

When I had my children, I was already a child therapist, schooled and trained to spot the enemy. I had lived with it, and I had studied it. I could see it a mile away.

And I did. One by one, in different forms and in different themes, it knocked on our family's door. Both girls took after me, my son getting a different flavor. It was hard to stomach, seeing my own fears mirrored back to me in stereo once again. I wanted to find the replay button and hit stop.

I was determined to not let anxiety or OCD hide, so fighting them became a family affair. We grabbed hold of that beast together. It became a family conversation, a family conquest. My kids are warriors, working hard to beat the genetic odds—and they're doing it. I had been a warrior too, and then somehow lost my footing and got stuck in the mud.

I grabbed a protein bar from the pantry and took a bite.

It tasted like sawdust and raisins. I reached for a cup of water to force it down.

"Are you working today?" Alex asked.

"Yeah, I'm sorry, I have to." She lowered her head into her cereal bowl. I felt a pang of guilt. "But when I get home we can go out for dinner," I said, trying to sound upbeat.

I worked two Saturdays a month. So much better than the early years when I had worked six days a week, clocking in sometimes more than 50 therapy hours at a stretch.

I went into our bedroom bathroom to brush my teeth. Jimmie was stirring, the light shining in through our blinds. We could never get our room dark enough, the light was always finding its way in. I wished that was the case now. I felt as if I was drowning in a sea of darkness. It had been three days since I fell into the darkness and there had been no reprieve, no ray of light signaling this was going to end any time soon.

Jimmie rolled over and slowly sat up. I stood there, mechanically moving the toothbrush back and forth as I gazed off into space. "Hey," he said as he rubbed his eyes. "How did you sleep?"

I stared back at him, lost in my own void. "Oh, okay, I guess," I said through a mouthful of toothpaste and water.

I had not shared with him what had triggered my sudden shift in mood and decided to keep him in the dark. I felt embarrassed, even at the thought of the incident that brought me to my knees. My emotions were so raw. It was a cringeworthy story and I was worried about being judged. I was scared that he might think it was such a minor incident and didn't warrant such a big response. I already felt stupid—stupid for what I had done, and stupid for how it played out. I didn't need someone I respected to chime in. I didn't have any more armor to protect me if he had judgment to throw my way too.

I didn't like attention focused on me, especially if the attention was negative or even worse, pity. So, I remained quiet, my strange behavior and emotions veiled in mystery.

He wasn't one to push. Not like me. I would have been all over him if he suddenly went from happy and content to depressed and robotic. But his avoidant personality was finally working in my favor. He had given me space, barely even acknowledging my sudden drastic mood change. I'm pretty sure that made me feel even worse. He was probably thinking that whatever it was, it would run its course and sputter out, eventually losing steam. But it was full steam ahead and there were no red lights in sight.

"Did I do something wrong?" he finally asked, tilting his head and raising his eyebrows.

I stared through him, surprised he was asking now. "No," I said, weighing the possibility of telling him what had happened. "I'm just upset about something," I confessed, avoiding his gaze. "I don't want to talk about it," I quickly added.

"Did the kids upset you?" he tried again, pulling at his ring nervously.

"No," I said, turning away and putting the shower on.

My mind was trapped in a fog I couldn't escape. If I wasn't going to talk to him, maybe I needed to find someone else to talk to. Finally, I said, "I think I might see someone," and then added, "I think I might need help." I scanned his face, analyzing his reaction for any signs of concern or worse, pity.

His face didn't reveal anything, it never did. No wrinkle of worry etched in his brow, no softening of the shoulders as he pulled me in for a tight hug. Just a quick nod and then, "Okay." And with that I sank deeper down, the darkness dimming the rest of my light. I opened the glass door of the shower and went in, washing off my body and my embarrassment.

I wanted to scream, *I am not okay!* I wanted to create a fire and give up my location, gather rocks and spell out SOS as clearly as I could. But asking for help was not in my DNA and if it ever was, it had been removed a long time ago.

As I drove to my office I thought about what I had said. Would I really go and see someone? Or had I only said that to wake my husband up, to get him to really see me. Lately I had felt so invisible around him.

I toyed with the idea of seeing someone, trying it on to see if it fitted. I had never seen anyone—ever. The irony was not lost on me, even in my foggy state. I had been in so many therapy sessions, more than I could count. So many for my father, so many for Leigh, so many for my children, so many for my clients, but none were ever for me.

Could I even stomach seeing a therapist? Would I be a chef in someone else's kitchen, analyzing the ingredients and critiquing the flavor? Would they think I was unprofessional, unworthy or overreactive? Would they judge me for doing something wrong, agreeing with the pack of wolves who had devoured me and left me in this state? Or, worse, would they think that it was no big deal, a trivial situation that they would have shrugged off, and look at me with pity? I was starting to think it was worth the risk to find out.

I unlocked my office and took in the smell of the orange-cranberry candle. It smelled like happiness and candy. My office always made me feel better. The solace, the peace and the silence were healing. I plopped my bag down and turned on all the lamps. As I stood by the coffee table, staring at the magnet balls stacked high in the air, I remembered my agreement with myself. *Oh yeah, who's next? Miss Ten.* I stared at the clock. *I have time, I should let her in.*

Miss Ten sat in one of the hallway foldout chairs, her back and shoulders slouching, making her small frame look even smaller. Her long brown hair flowed down nearly to her shoulders. Her young prepubescent body showed no hint of budding anytime soon. In the last few years she had grown taller, but her skeletal frame hadn't really changed. She looked somewhat disheveled. Her hair wasn't combed, and it lay wildly on top of her small head.

"Hi," I said, startling her. She looked up with a cautious smile, her eyes penetrating mine. She had already lost some of her innocence, leaving some of that early trust back at Washington Avenue. I didn't reach for her hand. I knew that would have made her uncomfortable, a sign of too much intimacy, something she wasn't used to. I smiled and nodded towards my office. "Let's go."

She walked in and sat down, picking up one of my squishies.

"These are cool," she said, putting the squishy to her nose to see if it had any scent.

"It lost its smell a few years ago," I explained. "But it never smelled that good anyway." I shrugged and took a deep breath. "So, let's dive in, shall we?"

She looked up and put the pineapple squishy down. "Sounds good." Her gaze met mine for the first time.

"So, how's it been going?" I asked, trying to start with something simple.

She grabbed a couch pillow and hugged it with both arms. "It's good. I really like Hall Academy. Fourth grade has been really fun. My teacher is nice."

I stared at her as she talked. She was animated and friendly. You could tell she really enjoyed having the attention on her, to have someone finally ask about *her*. But even at ten she had learned to keep things pretty simple, a painted facade of happiness dripping off her words.

"That's good to hear," I responded, mapping out where to go next. "How are the kids at Hall Academy?" I massaged the stress out of my neck.

"They're nice. I have lots of friends," she said, giving me another surface response.

I nodded, "How about Deanna and Gabriella or Grant and Brayce. Are you friends with them?"

She squirmed and brought the pillow closer to her chest before answering. "No, I don't hang out with them," she said, not elaborating any further.

We sat in silence for a few seconds. "Why?" I finally asked, putting my palms out, even though I knew her answer.

"They're in another group, so we don't hang out," she said, as she tightly clasped her hands together.

I knew where her pain points were just starting to take form. "Do you feel as if you fit in with them?"

She licked her bottom lip and paused before answering. "I guess not really," she said in a low tone.

I was relieved that she was starting to open up, so I pushed on, "Tell me what makes you feel that you don't fit in with them."

She repositioned her small body and tightened her grip on the pillow. "They seem like they've known each other for a long time. I think they all must have been friends forever. Also, I think they're all really rich too. We aren't rich, not even close. I just don't think they would like someone like me."

And there he was. He was small, and shaky on his feet, but Paro, her social anxiety, was learning how to take his first steps.

"Do you know much about their family background, like how they all met or where they all live?"

She looked up at the ceiling and then said, "I guess not. They just seem like they have lots of money. They all seem really close. I'm sure their families are friends. They probably hang out every weekend."

I paused for a second and then asked again, "But do you *know* this or are you *assuming* this?"

A small wrinkle appeared between her brow and her smile started to fade. I could tell she didn't like her assumptions being challenged. "I'm not assuming it. That's how they are," she said more firmly.

"That's what people do with social anxiety. They make a lot of assumptions," I said, putting my hands out.

Her eyebrows relaxed, as a small smile grew. "Social anxiety? Oh no, you've got me all wrong. I'm very social. Do you know I want to be an actress? I'm very outgoing. I'm the one who comes up with all the games at recess. I don't get nervous about making friends." She was sitting up straighter now.

"Sadly, people don't always understand social anxiety. They think it has to do with being shy or introverted, but in reality it is none of those things. You can be outgoing or friendly and have social anxiety. Some people are shy or more introverted, but you don't have to be in order to have social anxiety," I explained, thinking how she wouldn't describe herself as extroverted when she got older.

The wrinkle in her brow reappeared. "I don't get it. So then what is it?"

I continued, glad she was willing to keep discussing it. "Social anxiety is about the fear of rejection, the fear of being criticized or left out. It makes you think you don't fit in. It can make you over-analyze every social interaction. It can make you doubt everything. It can make someone so worried about embarrassment or rejection that they eventually just want to avoid social interactions altogether."

She let go of the pillow and placed it next to her. "Well, that's not me. I'm not worried about being left out. That's not my issue. There is a girl named Natalia in my class. Maybe she has social anxiety. Everyone leaves her out."

I looked at her knowingly, "You know, years later you might feel really bad about how you treated Natalia. You might even wonder why you were so cruel to her."

"I'm not cruel to her!" she said as she locked her arms together and shifted in her seat.

I softened my tone, "Let's have an honest conversation, shall we? You are cruel to her and, trust me, you will feel very bad about it for decades to come. But I want to dig deeper with you. Do you know why you are mean to her?"

She unfolded her arms and grabbed the pillow, a permanent frown now painted on her face. "No," she said flatly.

"Because she reminds you of you," I said. "Everyone tells you that she looks just like you. They call her your twin. Even her name is close to yours. How does that make you feel?"

I could tell that hit a nerve. She squeezed the pillow tighter. "I look nothing like her! I don't know why they say that. I am *nothing* like her."

I decided to push my luck and continue. "But really...you are. She is a mirror to your insecurities. Her family is poor and homeless. She is getting a scholarship to go to that school. She is friendly but scared. She's been to so many new places and had to meet so many new people," I explained. "So much of that is true for you too," I added softly.

She sat on the couch in silence, but her face softened.

"Okay. Maybe we are a little bit similar, but that doesn't mean I have social anxiety. Far from it actually," she said, quickly moving us away from Natalia and going back to our original discussion.

"Well, social anxiety often takes time to build. The seeds have been planted inside you and some small weeds are starting to grow, even right now, at your age," I warned.

"I don't see it," she said, shaking her head.

"As you get older you will enter every social situation in the exact same way you entered Hall Academy. Your social anxiety will quickly and efficiently divide people into groups. These are the popular people. These are the unpopular people. These are people who can be my friends," I explained.

"Yeah, but doesn't everyone do that? Isn't that kind of normal?" she argued.

"Yes, and that is a good point. It is normal to do that, but it's the level and intensity at which you do it. And it's the assumptions you make along the way. You fixate on the people who don't like you. You fixate on the people who are 'cooler' than you. You make up reasons why they don't like you. Instead of focusing on your friends, you focus on them. Instead of focusing on your fun, you focus on *their* fun. You start to tell yourself the same stories repeatedly. I'm not rich enough, smart enough, or pretty enough to be liked. Over time, you start to believe those lies, and social anxiety gets the upper hand."

She started to pet the fuzzy pillow on her lap. "But they don't like me. That's not in my head. They don't want to play with me. They don't try to talk to me," she whined.

"Yes, and that may be. But it's important to remember that not everyone is going to like you and that's okay. It doesn't mean that there is something wrong with you. You are a funny, smart, kind kid—but over time you won't believe that. You will need others to confirm your value. You will let others determine your happiness based on their acceptance of you."

That was a big concept for Miss Ten to comprehend. It is always hard to separate the forest from the trees when it comes to social anxiety. In fact, that's what makes social anxiety so impenetrable at times. You can't even see it when it's staring right at you.

It had been a hard session. I worried that I may have been a bit too direct with her. I tried to wrap it up with some softer words of hope.

"You know how your teacher told you that she believes you can be an actress?" I asked.

She looked up from the pillow, now covering half her face. "Yeah," she said.

"You may not wind up being an actress, but you are going to do something even better. Something that will help a lot of people just like you."

She smiled, dropped the pillow in her lap, and waved a hand at me. "Nah, I'm going to be an actress. You watch."

I winked back at her. "Well, who knows!" I shrugged, even though I really did. She had so much determination in her. I forgot I once believed in myself so ferociously.

I opened the door to my office and we said our goodbyes. "It was so nice talking to you," I said.

"You too," she replied. I wondered if that was really true. I had been so harsh with her. I called out to her as she neared the front door. "Oh wait, one more thing," I said, trying to collect my thoughts. "Sometimes things have to get worse before they get better. But they will get better. I promise." I wondered if I should have added that last part.

My heart ached for her. I wanted to run to her and give her a tight hug before she went on her way. I wasn't concerned about what she had been through, I was more concerned about what was to come.

Chapter 6
Then
Dumfries Road

It was the summer after fifth grade and we had just spent two months away at sleepaway camp, after moving to our fourth house on Dumfries Road. My mom, always the master negotiator, had managed to get us into sleepaway camp tuition free. It had been a reprieve, some normalcy sprinkled into our dysfunction.

We started to unpack the car while I blinked back tears; the reality of being home was hitting me hard. I missed camp already. I had felt so much acceptance at camp, as if I truly belonged. It was like a large blanket, warming up my insecurities. We had just dragged our heavy trunks into the living room when the smells of dinner made my mouth water. I instantly knew my mom had made my special meal, steak and sweet potatoes. We didn't usually get steak, that was for her and her alone, so when we did, it was a treat.

In between bites, we talked about what teachers we would get for next school year. "Is she nice?" I asked Jake, globing butter into my sweet potato.

"Yeah, you'll like her," he said, taking another bite of his salad.

My mom looked up from her plate, finally tuning into our conversation. "Oh, you guys aren't going back to Hall Academy," she said, sucking the juice off her steak bone. "We can't afford it and they won't give us another scholarship."

The pin to the grenade was pulled. She tossed it onto the table and waited for the explosion.

"Wait, what?" Leigh said, putting her fork down. "We aren't going back?" She swallowed hard, her voice sounding frantic. The rest of us stopped eating and looked up, shock and concern written on all our faces.

"No, we can't afford it," Mom said, avoiding our stares as she took another bite of her steak.

My stomach soured and I had a hard time swallowing the last bit of sweet potato still in my mouth.

"Where are we going to go?" I asked, the floor beneath my feet starting to shift, as I tried to balance myself.

"You guys will go to the schools that we are zoned for. Leigh, you'll go to Highland High School and Jake and Tash, you'll go to Fontaine Junior High. Allison, you'll go to the elementary school down the street."

I had never heard of these schools. We had been living in our safe little bubble, in our safe little school for two years.

Leigh burst out crying. "There is no way I'm going to Highland. You can't make me!" she wailed, her face red and wet with tears. She angrily pushed her chair back and ran to her room. I felt the same way on the inside.

I sat at the table staring at my mom in disbelief—disbelief

that she kept uprooting our lives, and disbelief that she never understood the devastation it caused. My father was at the sink, scrubbing the dishes. He wasn't part of this decision, or any decision for that matter, his mind permanently on hiatus.

Dinner was over. We all went to our rooms to quietly lick our wounds and wrap our brain around the latest challenge. I buried my head in my pillow, my emotions pouring out in the only place where it was allowed. I was tired of starting over.

I may have been naive about where we were headed, but Leigh was not. Fontaine and Highland were violent inner-city schools, where even the toughest kids had a hard time. We were all lambs to the slaughter and Leigh was going to be their first meal.

My mom got back into the car after dropping Leigh off at Highland and let out a big sigh. "Well, that was definitely rougher than I thought," she said. I sat in the backseat and rolled my eyes, annoyed at her late epiphany. She looked at the students walking around and added nervously, "I hope she'll be okay. She is definitely a fish out of water." And with that she put the car in drive and drove us to the junior high version.

Fontaine Junior High looked like a cement fortress, no warmth, just a sea of gray. I felt nauseous and I doubled over in the backseat getting ready to throw up. I moaned, "I'm not feeling well." I was hoping for some relief, preferably in the form of an exit strategy, a get-out-of-Fontaine-free card.

My mom peered into the rear-view mirror with a look of exhaustion and impatience. "You'll be fine," she said coldly, putting a Band-Aid on my bleeding wound. "You'll be with Jake. Just stick together," her eyes darted to Jake, silently pleading.

I felt a tightness around my throat and a sour taste in my mouth. My small frame couldn't take it anymore. I threw up my nerves all over the backseat. My mom dug in her purse for a tissue. "Here," she said. "Wipe your face before you go in."

My legs were shaky as I got out of the car. The walk up to the school seemed like a hike I wasn't prepared to take. I nervously turned around hoping Mom would see my panic, but her car was already gone. "It'll be fine," Jake said, reading the worry on my face, his voice less convincing than Mom's. We walked in silence, heading up the path towards the school.

The sounds of laughter, screaming and yelling bounced off the walls in a symphony of chaos. Elbows and book bags knocked me around, making me lose my footing. My eyes desperately scanned each room number as I passed. *Please be 205, please be 205*, I thought, searching for my home room. The hall was starting to spin, and my throat was closing. I had never seen so many kids before. Some people glared at me as I passed, others bumped into me on purpose. I crossed my arms tightly around my body for protection.

As I squeezed past a crowd of rowdy boys, I saw a teacher outside a classroom. A wave of relief washed over me. I walked up to her in desperation, "Do you know where 205 is, please?" I half asked, half begged.

Her bored stare was replaced with pity. "Right here, honey," she said as she pointed to her class.

* * *

Later that day, we all sat around the dinner table sharing stories. Leigh sat with her arms crossed and her jaw clenched. "I'm not going back," she said. "That school is literally a prison. Do you know the girls are all doing drugs in the bathrooms? Like right there on the counter for everyone to see. And these guys are running down the hall calling it 'waste' land instead of highland."

I looked up from my plate confused. "Wasteland? What is that supposed to mean?"

My mom and sister ignored me and continued to argue. My mom pointed her fork in her direction. "Leigh, you have to just give it a chance. This was only your first day."

"Fontaine wasn't any better," I piped in, commiserating with my sister. "I'm pretty sure I'm going to get beat up. This guy hit me on my head for no reason *and* he's in three of my classes."

They both stared at me for a second and then ignored me and continued. "Why can't we go back to Hall Academy?" Leigh pleaded.

My mother turned to Jake who was eating quietly. "How did you like it?" she asked, hoping to get one kid on her side.

"It's a hellhole," Jake said matter-of-factly as he put another bite of kielbasa in his mouth.

My mother sighed and turned away. "How about you, Allison? How was school today?"

"It was great!" Allison said. "I made a new friend and she lives a few blocks away from us."

I rolled my eyes and glared at my sister. "Yeah, that's because she gets to go to this cushy local school down the road. I'd make friends too if I was there." Jealousy oozed from my mouth.

My mother did what she always did when she knew she had made a mistake, she got angry and revised history. She angrily put her hands up in the air, as if she was surrendering. "You're all ganging up on me. This is what you said you wanted! You all complained about Hall Academy. You had asked to go to public school, you wanted more options, more friends. Now that you don't like it, it's all my fault? Give me a break!"

She had a way of spinning the truth and making us all dizzy. Had I asked to leave Hall Academy? I didn't think so. Mom often got me to doubt my experiences.

We argued that whole night and much of the next night as well, but our destiny had been sealed and Mom wasn't going to change her mind. I had a three-year sentence at Fontaine Junior High, and I would serve out the entire three years. Leigh also had a three-year sentence, but she wouldn't make it through her first year.

The next few years were rough all around. Leigh decided if you can't beat them, join them. She was in full rebellion mode and my parents could not contain her. Daily clashes at my house became a scene from the *Jerry Springer Show*. Stability was nowhere to be found. I spent those years alternating between being buzzed into psych wards to see Leigh or my dad. My mother nailed down Leigh's windows, but nothing could keep her contained. Highland had forever changed her. Our family was permanently fractured. After several visits to local treatment centers, Leigh was shipped off to Florida, to a boarding school for troubled youth. My parents were looking for an escape plan, a final exit strategy, and they found one. Leigh never fully returned, choosing to live in a foster home rather than come back to the dysfunction. Who can blame her?

My sister's sacrifice helped my brother dodge a bullet. He was not given a life sentence at Highland the way Leigh had been. Instead, he served one year at Fontaine and was then given the gift of going to Ballard High School, a school way out of our district, but worth every single mile. My parents were unable to stomach another kid going off a cliff.

I was left to survive on my own at Fontaine Junior High. Between my father's suicide attempts and my sister's runaway attempts, there was no more energy to deal with my small dramas. Up until then I had been able to keep the genetic seeds of social anxiety from fully sprouting, but Fontaine Junior High was the perfect incubator to nurture what would be my lifelong beast.

I was caught between worlds, in a social no man's land of acceptance. I was an outcast with the rougher kids. My innocence, naivety and nerdiness were a guaranteed social killer for anyone who associated with me. A risk no one was willing to take in a school where bravado kept you safe.

There was sadly no reprieve for me from the small group of kids who came from money. They clung together like a bunch of grapes, not wanting to be picked. They looked at my hand-me-down clothes, my awkward short hair and my nervous smile and deemed me a lost cause, an embarrassment they would rather not claim as their own.

I became a target for all sides, a place to get one's anger out. My Paro started to whisper and then shout from his new script. *You are a disgrace. No one wants to be friends with you.*

I learned what halls to avoid and would take long routes to avoid getting pushed around. I had three consistent bullies who got their power by offering me their daily dose of torture. Jake was able to get rid of one of them early on.

"Is that kid bothering you?" he asked.

"Every day," I mumbled. And with that he took care of it. Troy might have been intimidating to me, but he was a small kid to Jake, who was two years older.

"He won't bother you again," he said later that day. A wave of relief poured over me.

But there was a new Troy around every corner.

Apart from telling Jake about Troy, I never told anyone in my family about the troubles I had at Fontaine. I never told them about the isolation, the cruelty or the loneliness I felt. I never mentioned the fear I felt every morning walking up to the courtyard or the embarrassment I felt walking along those halls. I was ashamed. Ashamed that I was an outcast. Ashamed that I had attracted such disdain. Ashamed that no group had wanted to claim me as their own.

When I wasn't being picked on, I was being blatantly ignored by the small clique of popular kids who came from the other side of town. They wore designer clothes and talked about busy weekends of pool parties and trips to the mall. They seemed to have immunity from the struggles I was experiencing. They lived in a protected bubble, unscathed by the harsh environment around them. I was jealous and angry at the same time. Here were kids in a similar situation to me, only they were not just surviving, but thriving.

To be unseen was almost as bad as being bullied. I sat behind them as they laughed and shared jokes. I felt invisible. My social anxiety, Paro, seized the moment to make his prime-time debut, spewing the rhetoric he had started when I was at Hall Academy. *You're not cool enough for them. You are awkward and weird. They all come from money and your family has nothing. No wonder they don't even look at you. You would never fit in with them.*

Something was taking hold and it didn't feel good.

But there was a silver lining at Fontaine. Midway through the first year I met a girl of my ilk. I walked into Mrs. Booley's math class, head down, plopping into my seat exhausted. I turned to look at the directions on the board when I noticed a new face sitting next to me. She had the deer-caught-in-headlights look that I remembered so well from my first day of school. She was my twin, almost. Her pale skin was dotted with freckles and her short hair hung loosely over her face. She looked just as uncomfortable and awkward as me. I felt instant camaraderie with her. I saw that she was sinking, so I threw her a lifeline.

I tapped on her desk to get her attention. "Hey, are you new here?" I whispered.

Her scared eyes softened and her face relaxed. "Yeah, first day," she said. She seemed friendly enough, so I continued.

"Do you want me to show you around?" I offered.

She swallowed and let out a deep sigh of what seemed like relief, "Yeah, that would be great."

We walked to lunch together. I showed her what halls to avoid and gave her the skinny on all the cliques. She seemed appreciative of the lowdown on our new environment. I was an astute observer of the social hierarchies and pecking order of our school and I was excited to share my findings with someone.

Vanessa had recently moved in with her aunt, escaping some troubled childhood she never talked about. We both came from dysfunction neither of us cared to share. Instead, we passed notes between periods with the ferocity of prolific writers, spilling juicy details about every aspect of our day. My life at Fontaine had suddenly become lighter. I felt a sense of belonging, of purpose.

Vanessa and I were inseparable, both clinging to each other for survival in an otherwise inhospitable land.

* * *

A few months into seventh grade, Vanessa came to school with a scowl. "What's up?" I asked, feeling uncentered in my gut.

She repositioned her backpack and sighed, "I have to change schools."

I wasn't expecting that, and it caught me off guard. I started to feel dizzy and abandoned. I opened my mouth, but no words came out.

She continued, "And the worst part is, I have to leave next week."

My knees got weak. "But, but why?" I stammered, my mind racing.

"I don't know," she shrugged, her face blank.

I was annoyed by her lack of emotion, by her lack of fight. "Do you want to move?" I asked incredulously.

"No, of course not," she said, folding her arms around her small frame.

"Then tell your aunt you don't want to," I shrieked. I was feeling enraged for both of us. She just shrugged and kicked the dirt from her shoes. "It's fine," she said, seemingly resigned to the idea.

But it wasn't fine, at least not to me. My thoughts spun out of control. Who would I eat lunch with? Who would I stand with before school? Who would I talk to? I was consumed with self-pity and concern. I stared at Vanessa, wanting her to say more, but she was looking off into the distance, her mind already checked out, perhaps in protection mode.

The next week came before I was able to fully digest the news. I walked up to the concrete courtyard before school, groups of kids around the entrance. I walked past the circles of kids packed together in tight little exclusive bundles. I found our quiet corner where we used to stand, the two of us, alone but together. I felt exposed, awkward. I watched as everyone laughed and chatted, relaxed, surrounded by friends. I put my backpack down and crossed my arms trying to feel warmth and protection. I looked at my watch. *Welcome to my new mornings*, I thought, *only ten more minutes of torture*.

Vanessa and I stayed in touch but only for a little while. Her life was bumpy, with lots of curves, and she didn't have time to look back in the rear-view mirror to see where she'd been. A few weeks after she left I received a call from her.

"Vanessa!" I said, perhaps too enthusiastically. "How is the new school? Tell me all about it."

"It's going great!" she exclaimed. My stomach dropped and I felt my hand tighten around the phone. "You won't believe this, but I'm actually really popular!" she continued. "Can you believe that? I wore these leggings with stirrups my first day of school and all the girls thought I was cool."

"Oh," I said, nervously picking at my nails. "That's so good. I'm happy for you," I lied. She detailed all the new personalities and gossip at her school, but her voice was faint in the distance, my Paro too loud to drown out.

You aren't the same. Once Vanessa got away from you, she did fine. You dragged her down. She isn't a social reject like you. Look at her now, totally popular. That would never have happened to you.

I hung up the phone, an unsettling tightening starting to form in my chest. I wanted to be happy for her, I really did. But I felt alone, abandoned by my partner in crime. She had been vindicated and I was left to serve out my sentence all by myself.

I spent the next year at Fontaine alone, no early release for good behavior, no option for parole. My scars were getting etched into my soul, tattooed to my brain. My social anxiety grew to its full maturation, a tapeworm consuming its host, leaving nothing behind.

Eighth grade Texas history class had become a torture fest.

Mr. Howard was a young teacher with a lazy disposition. Instead of bringing history alive he made us read it from the textbook, word for word, every single day. It was tedious for most, but it evoked a *swimming-with-sharks* kind of fear in me.

He turned to the whiteboard, his dress pants drooping off his small frame. "Open to Chapter 8," he started, his voice monotone and soft. Half the room yawned in anticipation. My heart started to pound.

"We'll start here," he said, pointing to the seat closest to the door. A few students put their heads down waiting for their turn. I straightened up and started to count the seats. *Three, four, five, six, and then me.*

The closer my turn came, the louder Paro got in my head. *What if you can't pronounce a word? What if you look stupid? What if everyone laughs? What if you run out of breath like you did last time?* I started to feel nauseous, the rhythmic pounding drowning out the words of the boy in front of me. Desperate thoughts started popping up like they always did. *I could get up and leave? I could tell him I feel sick. That's not a lie, I do feel like barfing.* But as always, I remained paralyzed and stuck to my seat.

There was an awkward silence in the room and all eyes were on me. I had been so lost in my own thoughts I hadn't noticed when the other kid had stopped reading.

"Go on," Mr. Howard said, pointing at me.

"Sorry," I stammered, unable to hear my own voice above the cacophony of fears swirling in my head. I took a breath and began to read. "Although not recognized as such by Mexico, Texas declared itself an independent nation, the Republic of Texas..." I started.

But I couldn't hear myself read, I never could. Paro was loud and deafening. *How many more paragraphs do you have? Do you think he'll let you stop at the end of this page? Scan the page for big words. Do you see any coming? Spot them before you must read them. Go, go! Do it quickly before you get to the next paragraph.*

I started to run out of air. I hadn't paused to take a breath. I was reading the words, but I was running out of oxygen. *How much longer will he make me read?* The words floated above the book and I started to feel as if the room was spinning.

Paro saw the weakness and seized on the new opportunity. *You're going to pass out. You don't have enough air. You can't breathe. You can't read because you can't breathe.*

I started to hyperventilate. I paused at the end of the page, gulping in air like a fish washed up on shore. I waited for Mr. Howard to notice my distress and move on to the next kid.

"Go on," he said dryly, motioning with his hands, clearly annoyed by my pause.

I sucked in more air as the panic continued to grow. I started again, "Cotton, ranching and farming dominated the economy..." I stopped suddenly, pausing awkwardly in the middle of the sentence, running out of air again, "...this was a major factor in the development of new cities away from rivers and waterways."

I looked up for a second, mentally willing Mr. Howard to recognize my pain. *Please, let me stop.* He yawned and picked at his nails.

I reluctantly continued. Finally, after a few more minutes he looked up, wiped some chalk off his dress pants and said, "Next."

A wave of relief washed over me, and my racing heart started to hit the brakes. As the sounds of someone reading played in the background, I sat there, unable to focus for the remainder of class. The main event was over, but my Paro wanted us to attend the post-party celebration. *Do you think anyone noticed how out of breath you were? Do you think people saw how much you were panicking? You can't even read in class, what an idiot. Also, I'm pretty sure you mispronounced that one word.*

The bell finally rang and I stood up, feeling shaky and woozy from the flood of adrenaline and cortisol that dutifully came to my false alarm.

The rest of the night I would stay up worrying. Worrying about fourth period. Worrying about my turn. Worrying about my five minutes of panic and humiliation. It consumed my thoughts and devoured any joy. Fontaine had become a torture ground for my social anxiety.

Perhaps if I hadn't had the experience at Fontaine my social anxiety wouldn't have had the death grip it did in the years that followed. But in life we don't get the privilege to know what would have been, we only know what is.

Chapter 7
Now

My hands clenched the steering wheel as I tried to count my breaths in a weak effort to calm down. It's no big deal, I told myself. *It's good to get help and talk things through.* But my anxiety was in rare form that morning. *What a stupid thing to see someone about. There are so many bigger problems in the world than this.* I felt small, fragile and stupid. I contemplated turning around.

But the fog had not lifted, even though the weather should be good. I couldn't live like this for much longer; it wasn't fair to my kids, it wasn't fair to myself.

I sat on a small couch staring at the receptionist. A few minutes later a woman appeared. "Natasha?" she said, holding a folder with my name on it.

"Yup, that's me," my words came out soft and unsure.

"I'm Marty," she said with a smile, "come on back."

Marty was a bit smaller than me, her long blond hair swaying as we walked to her office.

"So, what brings you in today?" she asked, a warm smile on her face.

I sucked in air, gaining the strength to talk about it. "Well, something kind of minor and stupid happened, but I haven't been able to get over it. I'm worried because it kind of put me into a funk," I tried to explain, minimizing my dark days and depressive state down to "a funk."

"Well, nothing is minor or stupid if it has a big impact on us. What happened?" she asked.

I started at the beginning because I wanted her to understand why this small incident cracked the ground of my stability.

"I have social anxiety," I explained, touching my face self-consciously, "and I really thought I was working through it. I had done so much work." My mind flashed back to all the anxiety challenges I put myself through to show Paro who's boss.

"I always felt as if I was on the outside looking in, wherever I went. Every school I went to, every neighborhood we moved to—even as an adult, I felt that I didn't fit in." I noticed some of the heavy pressure on my chest starting to lighten as I talked. "Actually, I felt like even more of an outsider as an adult because I thought I would outgrow those feelings, but I never did," I said, looking down. "But I was finally putting myself out of my comfort zone. I was feeling more confident. I was trying to talk to my neighbors. I didn't feel as awkward standing in the school line to pick up my kids. I had become friendly with one neighbor whose child was in my son's class. It felt good to start to know people."

She looked at me with understanding eyes; I could tell she knew the story didn't end there.

"So, that neighbor told me there was a non-official Facebook group for our neighborhood. She asked me if I was in it. I told her no, I had no idea there was such a thing. Apparently, I was probably one of the only neighbors not in there, me and maybe the 85-year-old lady down the street." I sighed, took a sip of the Starbucks coffee I had brought with me, and continued.

"I remember going in that group for the first time and being shocked that there was this whole interconnected world of chatter coming out of my quiet neighborhood. It was eye opening. I felt as if I was late to the party. We had lived at that house for five years. But it was also unnerving. Most of the posts were innocuous and friendly, but a few made me cringe. A picture of someone's house with trash in front of it, with a nasty, shaming comment. A picture of someone's car with a post about how they were speeding."

She nodded and said, "It's amazing what people will post behind the comfort of a keyboard." I felt a wave of validation from her.

"So, one morning I was rushing around because I had a therapy session at 8:30 and I had no wiggle room between dropping my kids off and getting to my office."

I thought back to that day, as the most minute details were still etched in my mind's eye a month later...

"Come on!" I screamed from the stairs. "We have to go! I'm going to be late." I looked at my watch and my heart started to pound faster. "We need to go right now!" I barked, feeling the pressure of time closing in.

My daughter ran down the stairs and yelled, "I'm coming!"

I stared at my son, who was sitting at the bar eating breakfast. "We have to go NOW," I called in his direction. "Grab your shoes and get in the car. You can put them on when we are on the way."

He silently got up and put his bowl in the sink and grabbed his shoes. He knew I was in rare form. I had my momzilla moments and this was definitely one of them.

The kids piled into the car while I grabbed my work bag and my iPad, trying to hold my coffee with my other hand.

I balanced my coffee cup between my chin and my neck, as I tried to negotiate my way into the car. I took a deep breath and stared at the car clock. Doing good. I could still be on time. I realized I had been holding my breath and so I forced an exhale. I turned around and stared at the kids, who were unusually silent.

A pang of guilt hit my stomach. "I'm sorry I shouted," I said, looking back at them.

"It's okay, Mom," they said, almost in unison.

I put the car in reverse and pulled off our street on to the next one. Ahead of me was a school bus slowing down. I sighed. *Oh no, don't slow me down, please be turning.* I moved forward in an effort to pass it, but as soon as I started, the bus's stop sign was extended, and the red blinking lights flashed in warning. I hit the brakes and sat behind the stop sign, tapping the steering wheel anxiously. Every second felt like a minute. I watched the clock move as we remained frozen in time. My heart started to thud. I was definitely going to be late.

From the corner of my eye, I saw a man starting to cross the street. He made it halfway across when he stopped and paused in front of my car. He peered into the window and glared at me, his eyes cold and aggressive. My stomach automatically flipped nervously, feeling on edge. What was that about? Feelings of vulnerability and insecurity crept in. He turned away and continued to the other side of the road. It left me feeling uneasy and confused. *Was I being paranoid, or did he just give me a death glare?* I knew my anxiety often made me read into things, so I tried to shrug it off. *Maybe he was just having a bad day*, I lied to myself.

I didn't give the incident any more thought until later that evening. Dinner was made and I could hear the kids laughing upstairs. Jimmie was relaxing on the couch. I sat down to catch a breath and relax as well. I grabbed my iPad and plopped it on my lap. It had been a long day of sessions and my mind was mush and my body ached. My fingers haphazardly went to Facebook to mindlessly look through the feed.

I was scrolling on automatic pilot when something caught my attention. It is one of those moments when your subconscious knows there is an issue before your conscious mind recognizes it. My hands instantly got clammy, and my mouth felt like sandpaper. *Wait, what was that?* My mind whispered, *Scroll back.* There in the middle of the feed was a picture of my car behind the bus from this morning. The room started to spin, and a shakiness started to rock inside of me. Oh my God, is that a picture of me? My eyes darted to the thread. "Whoever drives this car is a fucking moron who should have their license revoked. A 16-year-old drives better than that. I'm sick of people not stopping. At least this one stopped, which is better than some, but come on, people!" My legs started shaking and soon my whole body was in tremors. I felt enraged and embarrassed at the same time.

My body was responding to a five-alarm fire. Adrenaline raced throughout my body and the room went sideways. I sat on the couch, unsure of what to do or how to respond. My hands hovered shakily over the keyboard, frozen in mid-air. It was hard to focus, and I realized I had been holding my breath. I exhaled forcefully and angrily typed out, "Wow. Thanks for taking my picture!" and slammed my hand down on the return button.

Looking back, I wish I hadn't done that. Would it have been better if I had just apologized and moved on? "So sorry I didn't stop 20 feet behind the bus. I'll do better next time." Would that have stopped the onslaught of wolves from eating me whole or would it have happened anyway?

The avalanche started with just a rumble as I tried to explain myself. "I'm sorry, I thought the bus was turning," I typed, feeling instant remorse at what I had initially typed. But in the world of the internet, the mob mentality is part of the culture, and the mob was at my front door.

"No, you didn't!" one wrote. "Clearly the bus wasn't turning."

"She's an idiot!" another piped in.

They were ruthless. If it had been just an anonymous Facebook group I would have removed myself and tried to move on. But these were my neighbors, people in the community, parents whose children went to school with my kids. I had to defend myself.

My body was shaking so much I was practically convulsing.

I felt an anxiety attack inside me erupting. I was starting to have a hard time catching my breath.

I typed again, "I apologize. Yes, I was in a hurry, and I should have slowed down sooner. I admit that I made a mistake and I promise to be more careful next time. But I think we also need to talk about these things with more respect. Calling someone a 'fucking moron who should get their license revoked' isn't the way we should talk to each other. I wouldn't want any of our kids to handle their problems like that."

Mistake #2. I probably shouldn't have done that. It was like waving raw meat in front of an already hungry pack.

The comments poured in.

"Where does she live?"

"I think she lives on my block, and I am pretty sure she has kids of her own!"

"Unbelievable."

"Can we call the cops on her? Maybe she can get charged?"

"We don't need people like that in our neighborhood."

It was an avalanche now and it seemed that there was nothing I could do to stop it. I typed more to defend myself. It was like trying to get out of quicksand, my efforts pulled me further down.

"I should have stopped sooner, but you can see from the picture that I clearly stopped. Yes, I am not 20 feet back, but I am behind the stop sign. I admit I was having a bad day and I should have stopped sooner. I recognize that and apologize for that but attacking someone in such a cruel and malicious way is uncalled for."

I sat back, waiting for someone to come to my defense. I was so naive.

"Are you serious? You are going to turn the table and make this about us? YOU are in the wrong. YOU put our kids in jeopardy. Don't make this about how we talk to people, that's ridiculous!"

I tried to walk away from the keyboard. I went to the bathroom to try and calm myself down. My stomach was having a torrential storm, swirling the rest of dinner, sending waves of nausea throughout my body. I felt panicky that I had just walked away from the conversation. What are they saying about me now? I rushed back to my iPad, concerned I had walked away only to get sucker punched.

"Unbelievable. Something needs to happen to these people!" someone posted.

"That is so appalling!" wrote another.

It seemed as if every few seconds someone new saw the picture and joined the ever-growing pack of angry wolves.

This went on for hours, hours. As angry comments poured in, my friendly neighbor, with whom I thought I had developed a friendship, was nowhere to be found. No kind words to rescue me. I felt abandoned, naked on stage with no one willing to pull the curtain. I felt like a criminal. I felt as if I had murdered someone. I replayed the morning over and over in my head until I convinced myself that I was a horrible person.

A few brave strangers started to pipe up, people I will always remember for taking a few seconds out of their day to help someone they didn't know.

"Leave her alone already. She doesn't need to wear a scarlet letter for this."

"I think we should move on," added another.

"Hasn't she had enough?" one pleaded.

But for every brave comment, came a litany of attacks. It seemed never ending. I tried again, thinking maybe I could salvage this.

"All I am saying is that people will make mistakes. But we can talk about this calmly, without being cruel. That's how I would want my kids to handle conflict."

But I probably should have stopped. No, I definitely should have stopped. Any comment I made was like pouring fuel on an already blazing fire, and I was the biggest casualty.

"Mistakes! Mistakes! You could have killed our kids," one person wrote.

I stopped commenting. There was nothing I could do to stop the onslaught of attacks. I just needed to play dead and get it over with.

My messenger box dinged.

"Hi, you don't know me, but I am sorry for the way they are treating you. That's not right," someone wrote.

I typed back, my hands still shaking, "Thank you. I appreciate that."

Another message arrived from another unknown neighbor.

"So sorry for what is happening. You handled yourself so well amid all those attacks. I learned a lot from you tonight," she wrote.

A small flutter of relief came over me. It was nice to see a few people who were able to separate themselves from the pack and be human.

After about six hours, the thread started to lose its speed.

* * *

I looked up at Marty, scanning her face for any condemnation. Would she have to hide her scorn? Over the past month, I had replayed that incident hundreds of times in my mind, each time convincing myself more and more that I was a horrible person.

"That's unbelievable," she said, shaking her head. "It's disgusting the way they treated you."

I exhaled, her words washing over me, cleaning the grime off my conscience. I reached over to take a sip of my cold coffee, remembering the days that followed that night, and I began to recount them to Marty...

* * *

The next morning, I felt as if I had an emotional hangover. I had to get the kids ready for school and didn't have time to lick my wounds or wallow in self-pity. I quickly opened my iPad and went to Facebook, my heart starting to quicken as I scanned the page. Nope, no more comments. Relief washed over me.

Robotically, I moved about the house, putting waffles in the toaster and pouring milk absent-mindedly. I took Chloe to school first. As I drove back towards the house my hands tightened around the wheel. I started to have a hard time catching my breath, an invisible chokehold silently suffocating me. I started to panic. I inhaled sharply, trying to force my lungs to expand. I was getting closer to the street where the bus had stopped. *What if people are waiting there? What if I must stop? Will that man glare at me? Will he confront me? Will everyone recognize my car and take more pictures, mocking me?* My throat got dry, and it was hard to swallow. The incident had reignited my social anxiety, like a spark on a pile of old, forgotten dynamite. It was all my fears and insecurities delivered on a silver platter. *People will judge you. People won't like you. You are on the outside looking in,* my Paro had mocked. And now my reality and my fears had merged into one. Paranoia was replaced with facts.

I turned the corner and gave an audible sigh of relief when I saw no one on the street. The tremble in my hands started to dissipate and I pulled into my driveway.

I walked into the house and was short tempered with my kids. "Let's go," I said, all business-like. Xander and Alex piled into the car, laughing at a joke I didn't hear. I grabbed their backpacks and put them in the backseat as I threw my own bag into the front.

I put the car in reverse and pulled out of the driveway, starting to feel my throat close again, my breath getting shallow. *It's fine. You need to just calm down. You are making a mountain out of a molehill.* But my body refused to cooperate. I turned the corner of our street, holding my breath. All clear. Almost there.

I stared at every car that went by, watching the driver, scrutinizing their response. *Did they stare at me? Did they recognize me?* The spotlight I had felt with social anxiety was now magnified.

The school drop-off lane wasn't any better. Every glance, every look in my direction was proof that the world was now conspiring against me. Everyone seemed in on the joke and I was the punchline. If my social anxiety was a small gnat before, it had suddenly morphed into Godzilla, and it was swallowing me whole.

I started to panic. *I can't do this. I can't drive this car around.* It was like parading around with a sign that said, "It was me. I did it! I'm the one you were mocking." I craved anonymity. I wanted to blend in like a chameleon on a green leaf. I wanted so desperately to just disappear.

I tried to reason with myself. *That's avoidance. You've worked way too hard on your social anxiety to slip backwards. You don't avoid. You do the opposite of avoid. You face your fears. You hold your head high.* But my words of encouragement fell flat.

I contemplated trading the car in. I thought if I could get rid of the evidence, I could bask in the pool of anonymity once again. *People are noticing the car, not me. Get rid of the car and everything will be so much better.* My brain fought with itself. *No! That's avoidance.*

Fine! I shouted silently. *I won't trade the car in. But this feeling isn't going away anytime soon.*

* * *

"And it didn't," I explained to Marty. "The feelings just stuck around, digging me further and further into this hole."

Marty nodded her head, seeming to understand the impact it had on me. She took a breath and then said, "The problem is you thought you could change people, but instead they just wound up dragging you down." I nodded in agreement, feeling their pull even now. "You can't shine light when people are craving darkness. In those moments, you just have to remove yourself before you get swallowed up."

I let her words sink in for a while. She was right, it had been like trying to swim upstream through a raging river, an impossible feat. "I know," I said. "I don't know why I even tried. I just didn't like the idea that people thought I was a bad person," I shrugged.

After the session, Marty walked me out of her office. I felt lighter, more myself again. It had been nice to unload some of that weight. I scheduled a few more sessions with her. I thought to myself, *Maybe this will be the light that will help get me out of this darkness.*

* * *

I stared at the candle next to my chair, watching the fire dance in silence. It was time to talk to Miss 14. It was getting tougher. I wondered if this process was even necessary. Wasn't I getting better? Did I really have to keep doing this?

No, I told myself. *You started this, you must finish it.* I was always a sucker for seeing everything through to completion and this was no exception.

I got up slowly and walked to the door, worried about who I would meet on the other side. It wouldn't be the innocent ten-year-old I said goodbye to a few days before. I poked my head out of the door, not wanting to fully commit. I could see her sitting there, uncomfortable and awkward, pulling on the thread of her pants. Her hair was cut in a short, unflattering style.

"Hey, come on in," I offered, as I opened my door a bit wider and waved her over. She slowly got up and gave me a cautious smile, braces guarding her tongue. I smiled back, trying to soften the mood.

We sat down in silence, both of us enveloped by the smell of my orange-cranberry candle.

"So, how was your last year at Fontaine?"

She gave me a half smile and said, "It was okay," not elaborating any further, politely waiting for me to continue the conversation. I knew how she felt, because I had felt it a million times before. The thought that it would be too rude, too indulgent to fill the room with facts. Too narcissistic and self-absorbed to ramble on without another invitation.

"I mean it, how is it *really* going?" I asked again, giving her permission to focus on herself.

She sat back on the couch and got more comfortable. "Well, it was hard after my friend Vanessa left," she said, looking down to pick at her clothes. "She was really my only close friend there."

I remembered the intense loneliness I felt at the time. The uncomfortable feeling of having no one in a sea of cliques. She was definitely downplaying it.

"I know it was hard to not have any friends and even harder when you felt as if you didn't fit in," I said, trying to have a more honest conversation with her.

She squirmed in her seat and said, "It was okay." I knew she didn't like to be pitied.

"You know that Fontaine really was a tough school. Anyone would have issues there," I said, trying to offer comfort.

She looked up from the invisible thread she was pulling on her jeans. She stared at me with what looked like a combination of appreciation and cynicism. "Other people seemed to do just fine," she said dryly.

"I know you felt as if there was something wrong with you, but there wasn't," I said, leaning closer to her. "Fontaine was a rough school and there was no way you were going to fit in, not from that small, sheltered school you came from," I explained.

"It was a rough school," she agreed. "And I don't blame those kids for not wanting to hang out with me." She looked down at her feet. "We came from different worlds. I'm sure I seemed way too sheltered for them. I get it," she said, staring off, lost in thought. "It's the other kids, the ones who seemed sheltered like me," she finally said. "They made me feel like such a loser," she whispered, barely audible.

My heart ached for her; the loneliness and isolation was plain to see. "Have you ever thought that the deck was stacked against you?" I suggested. "Your family was in chaos. Your father was suicidal. Your sister was being sent away. The last thing you cared about was how you looked or what clothes you wore. Even if you did, there was no way your family could afford clothes that would have helped you fit in with those kinds of kids. It wasn't going to happen." I was trying to get her to see the bigger picture. "No one in your position was going to be accepted into that group. No one," I repeated.

She didn't respond. She sat quietly for a minute, perhaps

replaying my words in her mind, seeing if they were words of comfort or words of truth.

"I guess you're right," she finally said, with a touch of sadness in her voice. "I wasn't from their world either."

"No, you weren't," I agreed.

"I'm sure it will be better next year. My mom said she'll get me into Ballard instead of Highland, like she did for my brother. That seems like a good school. I'm sure I'll find friends there," she said.

I looked away, the memories of Ballard flooding back. "Yeah, I'm sure it will be great," I lied, trying to sound convincing.

We ended our talk and I walked her down the hall. I could tell she felt lighter than when she came in. We stood by the glass doors that led to the parking lot. "Listen," I said, turning towards her for the last time. "Fontaine triggered some emotions in you that might be hard to shake off," I tried to warn. "You have developed perceptions and insecurities that are pretty deep rooted."

She nodded in agreement. "I know," she said quietly. She opened the door and headed for the parking lot.

As I watched her walk away I thought about it. She really didn't know. It had been a perfect storm of environmental triggers and genetic seeds desperately looking for a way to grow. Her social anxiety had been fed, watered and encouraged to grow those last few years. There was no stopping it now.

Chapter 8
Then

Tooley Road

By the time I was 13 we had lost our car, we had lost Leigh, and eventually we lost our house on Dumfries Road. My parents were spiraling out of control. Leigh now permanently resided in another state and my parents moved on to the next problem.

As my father's business crumbled, so did his mental state. It was now commonplace for him to take short sabbaticals to places that locked him and his problems away.

* * *

We were off to camp, something my parents always managed to finagle, regardless of how unstable home life had become. My mother had the camp director's number on speed dial and wasn't afraid to use it.

Sleepaway camp always pumped some air into my deflated life. It was my haven, a reprieve from the grind. I loved the idea of recreating myself. There were no cliques or groups to break into, no pre-established opinions of me. I was free.

I met kids from all walks of life and was exposed to styles and music I had never heard of before. These kids didn't want to fit in, in fact it seemed like they went out of their way to do the opposite. I wanted to soak up their coolness, box it up, and bring it back home with me.

My social anxiety took the summer off, and I felt emboldened and confident.

At the summer sleepaway camp, they took the kids on a tubing trip down the white rapids. We all piled into a hot bus and sang songs as we made our way through the winding roads to the top of the river.

We sat bored and antsy as the man running the tubing company spoke. "So, if you find that you are headed straight for a rock, put your feet out and propel yourself forward. The rapids will keep you moving. Got it?" We all nodded, sweltering in the summer heat.

We grabbed large tubes and waddled to the river, like ants carrying giant crumbs on our back. People were scattered around the riverbank. Some were listening to music; some were having a summer picnic. It was a beautiful, ocean-blue-sky kind of day.

The rapids were faster than I anticipated, and I felt a sudden surge of panic. I flew down the river like a piece of driftwood, bobbing to the left and right as the water turned. After a few sharp turns, I told myself to just let go and feel the exhilaration of the wind and water spraying on my face. And I did. The thrill felt so good until I looked up and saw I was heading for a large rock. The water whipped around me, taking me right to it. The panic came flooding back. I tried to lean on the tube to steer away from the rock, but it didn't work. Everything slowed down and a flash of what the tube guy had said replayed in my head.

Foamy whiteness temporarily blinded my sight. I bent my knees and pushed off the rock but I felt an unexpected jerk from my right leg.

My heart pounded in my ears. I knew something wasn't right. My foot was stuck in a crevice. I feverishly yanked to get my foot loose. A white wave came crashing into the rock. I held my hands up defensively and my inner tube went flying up over my head. I gasped and choked as my head went under water.

Everything went silent and there was a steady buzzing in my ears. The rushing water, the music and the laughter became muffled. The waves started to pull at me, trying to move me forward without my tube. My body was being dragged in front of the rock, but my lodged ankle was holding me back. As my head bobbed up and down, I could hear the popping of my ankle ligaments. Waves of nausea hit me.

A thought started to grow louder than my panic. *Do something! If your ankle fully breaks, it will slip out of that crevice and you'll go down those rapids without a tube!* I saw a small stick poking out from the rock. I leaned all my weight forward, trying to reach it. I gently pulled the rest of my body forward, moving closer to the rock and out of the current. *Good.* The pressure from my ankle let up and I hugged my body close to the rock, one hand tightly holding the stick. I tried again to yank my ankle out of the crevice, but I couldn't do it without moving back into the current.

I was a small speck in the river and with the rushing waves

and constant activity, no one noticed me. I gulped in river water, as I tried to look over at the shore. There were people drinking beers, sunbathing, and listening to music. They seemed so close and yet they might as well have been miles away. I sat there for a few seconds frozen.

Now what? I was paralyzed.

Shout! Shout and ask for help! But when I opened my mouth, nothing came out. I sat in the water, my world caving in, my mouth offering no words to save me. I couldn't scream. I couldn't make a scene. I couldn't be a spectacle. I couldn't be a victim who needed help. It was mortifying. My social anxiety had such a death grip on me that even in a life and death situation, I couldn't break loose.

I stared at the stick. It was starting to fray. I knew once that stick broke, I would be flung back into the current and my ankle would completely break. I would be free from the rock, but I'd be flung into the rapids without a tube.

Scream! I barked at myself. *Scream now, you idiot! What are you waiting for?* I sucked in some breath and tried to find my voice. Finally, I pushed the words out of my mouth. "Help!" my voice was meek and hoarse. "Help! Please!" I tried again, my head bobbing up and down as I tried to look at the shore. No one looked my way, not even a glance. *Come on! I'm over here.* But time was running out. *Scream louder! Screw your embarrassment, who cares what people think!* I was growing desperate and scared. I was starting to lose sensation in my right foot. "Help!" I screamed, this time in a high-pitched panic. "Help, I need help!" I screamed louder, my voice growing more frantic with each plea.

Finally, people on the banks of the river heard me. "Hey, I think she needs help!" a shirtless guy said, a can of beer in one hand, as he pointed at me with the other. More people noticed.

The growing chaos caught the attention of the camp lifeguards who were a bit further down. They grabbed their life preservers and started heading down the riverbank in my direction.

One of my favorite camp counselors started to swim in my direction. He was a strong swimmer, and he was able to make it to me before the lifeguards did. He took his body and blocked the current, giving me an extra layer of protection. "Hang on," he said. "We'll get you out of there."

A few minutes later two lifeguards showed up next to him. They worked together to pull my ankle out of the crevice. They created a makeshift contraption with rope and a few inner tubes to get me to the other side. I was carried into a van and taken to the hospital.

During the van ride, they talked about the rescue like football players after a hard game. I was quiet and in pain, their voices faint in the background. I felt that I had let myself down. Why hadn't I been able to scream for help? The ever-growing swell of my ankle upset me, but my reaction disturbed me even more.

It was a bittersweet ending to an amazing summer. A summer that not only taught me about friendships but revealed something about myself. Something I didn't want to see. Paro wasn't only an inconvenience; he could be life threatening—something that I would see during another nail-biting moment in the future.

* * *

When we returned from camp we packed up our bags and moved to our fifth house on Tooley Road, away from the sorority of neighbors my mom called her friends. This time we rented a house due to my parents' credit and luck running out.

It was the start of my freshman year and I had dodged a bullet by securing a spot as a student at Ballard High School. Mom found a loophole that allowed students to attend if they wanted to join Future Farmers of America, a student organization for those interested in agriculture.

I felt free. Free from the fear that had consumed me at Fontaine and free from the social rejection and judgment that had become a part of my life.

I feverishly joined every club and after-school program I could access. I wanted a fresh start, and I knew I needed to put myself in more social situations. I carefully picked out my outfits to be as "cool" as I could on a limited budget. I tried to force myself to be friendly to people around me.

But by my second month I grew disappointed. No magic had happened. No warm, welcoming clique let me into their fold. My social anxiety didn't drip off me like a discarded shell after a spectacular metamorphosis. No. I floundered, stuck in my chrysalis, trapped and unable to see change.

As I was walking through an empty courtyard an older football player walked towards me headed in the opposite direction. As he got within earshot he looked at me and whispered, "Loser!"

A shot of acid hit my stomach and I felt unbalanced for a second. *Why did he say that to me?* His words derailed me. Paro had a field day with the situation. *See! Even at this school you are a loser! People can smell loser on you. It doesn't matter what you wear or how you act, you repel people, and no one will ever like you.*

I felt empty. My hope for a brand-new start was quickly fading.

* * *

For some reason, I was put in advanced history at Ballard. I had managed to survive history class with Mr. Howard, but I certainly hadn't excelled. And yet, there I was, in my only advanced class in ninth grade.

I didn't feel as if I belonged. Paro got warm and cozy. *Uh oh! Someone messed up. You shouldn't be here. Why are you in advanced history? That's a joke. You could barely read last year. This is going to be a torture fest part two, the sequel.*

I did little to fight back. I took Paro's sucker punches and added a few of my own. *It's true,* I agreed. *I don't belong here. It's only a matter of time before everyone realizes I am an outsider.*

Surprisingly, I managed well in the class. My teacher didn't make us read and for that I was eternally grateful. I was carrying a solid A and was starting to grow more confident, feeling as if perhaps I was honor level material after all. Maybe I was wrong. Maybe Paro was wrong. Maybe my family was wrong. I always felt as if they devalued my potential and didn't take me seriously.

And then one day, Mrs. Slotter took an axe and chopped down my small, but rapidly growing self-esteem. Through the murky fog of my thoughts, I heard her say, "Natasha!"

I straightened up and looked at her. "Sorry, what?" I said, stumbling on my words. She had never called on me before and I was startled by the sudden spotlight.

"Pay attention! What do you think the answer to number 8 is?" a smirk of satisfaction formed on her face.

As if on cue, Paro orchestrated a cacophony of emergency alarm bells in my body, and they were all going off at once. Enter racing heart. Bring in dizzy. Where is nausea? He is needed on stage.

My mouth went dry as I scanned the page to look at the question. "Um," is all I got out before she interrupted.

"You need to focus! Number 8 is asking about..."

Her voice trailed off, Paro easily drowning her out. *Oh my God! How stupid are you? Everyone thinks you are an idiot. Everyone is staring at you.*

But then Paro suddenly stopped shouting. I was jarred and confused by the sudden silence until I heard it for myself, "Okay, now YOU tell me what the answer is to number 8!"

Oh crap! I hadn't been paying attention. Paro had been too deafening. "It is, well..." I stammered yet again, the room starting to spin.

"You've got to be kidding me. The answer to number 8 is..."

As soon as she started talking, Paro boomed in my ear. *Dumb! Dumb! Dumb! Now people are really going to think you are an idiot.*

But Mrs. Slotter's fun was not over. "So, now you tell me

what I just told you." Her smirk had formed into a Cheshire Cat grin. She seemed to be enjoying this.

"I'm sorry, I don't..." I started to say. This time there was a loud audible gasp from the peanut gallery; the students were growing annoyed by me. I couldn't blame them. I was annoyed with myself.

The third time, I made sure to listen. I told Paro to shut up and I focused on her every word. I needed this to end. I was melting under her spotlight, and I couldn't take it anymore. I spat her words back to her and held out a white flag for a cease fire.

That memory is fused in my brain. I think about how I was made to feel naked and exposed, vulnerable and weak. I think about how my small, ever-growing self-esteem was ripped out of the ground, roots and all, guaranteeing no further sprouting that year.

I didn't have to wallow in my new reality for too long. Shortly after that incident, my parents left me and my siblings at their friend's house as they went back east for a visit. It was odd because my parents never went on trips and had never left us with anyone else.

A few days into our stay my mom called.

"Hey, Mom," I said, as I dangled the phone cord in my hand and held a popsicle with the other. "How's your trip going? When are you guys coming back?" I asked.

"Our trip is going well," she said. "We've decided we are going to move back to New Jersey," she blurted out, with no warning or preparation.

I was silent, deafened by the unexpected grenade. My hand tightened the cord around my fingers until it cut off my circulation. "Wait, what?" I was still trying to process her words. "When?" I finally asked.

"We'll come back, pack up, and then we'll go," she said, revealing her speedy timeline.

I hung up the phone, the popsicle dripping on the floor.

"What's wrong?" My mom's friend asked, staring at my expression.

"I guess we're moving," I said, dazed.

My mother remained true to her word. They arrived back home, we packed up our house on Tooley Road, and said goodbye.

Jake, fed up with riding shotgun on all my parents' poor choices, decided to jump ship. "I'm not going," he said matter-of-factly. "I'll find someone to stay with, but I'm not leaving." His tone dared them to challenge his decision. But there would be no push back, no parental boundary set this late in the game. That simple declaration was enough to leave my brother behind. He would finish up his junior year without us.

With no foresight or plan, we moved back to New Jersey and into my grandmother's home. My favorite childhood memories of Friday night dinners and comfort food were quickly replaced with discomfort and change.

My mother drove past my new school. "Isn't it beautiful?" she said, staring out her window.

I felt as if I was on another planet, uprooted from all that was familiar. "It looks like an Ivy League college," I said, underwhelmed, staring at the green manicured lawns and the stone brick buildings. "Is that really a middle school?" I asked, annoyed, knowing I would never fit in at a school like that.

We weren't returning to the modest, working-class town where we used to live. That would have been too easy. Maybe I would have connected with some friends from Washington Avenue. But no, for some reason, my parents decided to plant our roots a few towns over on West End Avenue, where the gross median income was ten times more than what they made.

To make things worse, ninth grade was considered middle school, so to add salt to my wound, I was getting a demotion.

We parked the car at the front of the school and walked up the small path to the front office next to the large sign that read Peak Middle School. "Are you excited about your first day?" Mom asked.

I stared at her, my face an olive shade of green. "Um, no," I said, trying to keep down the small breakfast I had just eaten. I was wearing a sweater and jeans I had painstakingly picked out. A white bow was holding up my hair and my self-esteem.

"So, you just need to sign here and here," the middle-aged lady in the front office said to my mom as she pointed to the sheet, "and then she should be set. Just give me a sec and I'll make a copy of these forms for you." She walked over to the copier.

The woman returned. "To make your first day a little easier, we are going to buddy you up with a girl in your grade. I'm sure she'll love to show you around. We'll call her to the office." And with that she picked up the phone and mumbled some instructions to the person on the other line. Holding her hand over the phone's mouthpiece she said, "She'll be down in a moment."

The knot in my stomach loosened a bit. I felt thankful for the social training wheels. I wasn't ready to ride on my own. I was exhausted by all these new starts.

I saw a girl about my age, walking down the corridor, looking as if she was coming to the office to get expelled. *Please don't let that be her, please don't let that be her.*

"Hey, Carla," one of the ladies behind a desk called out. "Thanks for doing this, hon," she said, "I owe ya one."

Shit. I looked at Carla and smiled. She had dirty-blonde hair sprayed a few inches off her head. Her blue eyes, heavily lined in black, glared at me and she didn't smile back. The knot in my stomach instantly got retied.

"Would you mind taking her around with you?" the lady enrolling me said.

"Sure, no problem," she said, her words and her expression mismatched. And with that, we left, me following behind like a lost puppy dog.

She barely said two words to me as we walked down the hall. "It's lunchtime, so I'll show you the cafeteria," she said, in a flat tone. We walked into a small lunchroom and she heaved her backpack onto the table. "I'm starving," she said to her friends.

There was a group of kids sitting at the table, all sporting the same Jersey look. They looked up and stared at me. "Who's that with you, Carla?" one of the girls asked.

"Oh, this is..." she started. "What's your name again?"

I could feel some heat on my cheeks. "I'm Natasha," I said, with a small smile.

"This is my best friend Sara," she said as she pointed to a petite girl with long blonde hair. "And this is Hilary and her boyfriend Jack," she said, pointing to a couple at the end of the table. The boy gave me a friendly wave, but the girl just glared at me, her acne-spotted face showing a scowl.

They all continued to eat their lunch as I sat there, a deer caught in headlights. I didn't know how to jump into a social situation. I didn't know how to develop new friends; I just knew how to feel awkward. No one asked me any questions or directed their conversation my way. I was, for all intents and purposes, invisible. A feeling I knew all too well.

I thought maybe people needed time to warm up to me, but things did not improve. This was a small town, and these friendships began in diapers and sippy cups. I was an outsider, and no one was jumping at the bit to invite me in.

Lunchtime became increasingly uncomfortable. I had nowhere else to sit, but it was obvious that I was becoming a burden to this group. Carla spent lunch with her back towards me, whispering in Sara's ear. My presence was a source of contention, and they weren't trying to hide it at all.

Lunch had become more than intolerable; it had become physically painful. I just couldn't stomach it anymore, but I didn't know what else to do. I had no friendships on the horizon and no other place to sit. All the students had to stay in the cafeteria, which meant no roaming the halls and no visits to the library. It was the cafeteria or the bathroom and that was it.

So, I did what any other sane person would do—I chose the bathroom.

Those were some of the most painful and awkward 35 minutes of my life. As everyone went to the cafeteria, I made my way to the furthest bathroom down the hall. I sat in the stall, my feet pulled up on the toilet seat, so no one would see me. I held my knees and took shallow breaths so no one would hear me breathing. It was a new low, and Paro didn't miss a beat. *Even here you can't fit in. You've run out of excuses. You were hand-delivered friends on a silver platter, and you still wound up alone.*

I felt like a ghost at that school.

I never told my family about my struggles. My parents were having their own issues. The cracks in my dad's foundation were growing into fissures.

Chapter 9
Then

West End Avenue

My parents eventually found jobs, my dad as a dental technician and my mom as an office manager. Stability was making a guest appearance in our lives. We rented a tiny white house on West End Avenue, a few towns over from my grandma's house. We all crammed into the small space. Jake begrudgingly rejoined the dysfunction for his last year in high school and Leigh was back from her childhood exile to start living her adult life. I was given the deja vu experience of being a high school student yet again.

A few months into my sophomore (second) year I started to finally make friends. My social anxiety brought with it many debilitating issues, but one small perk was my keen sense of observation. I noticed everything. I could tell the social hierarchy of a room within the first glance. I could tell who liked who, who wanted to date who, and who was on the outside looking in, just like me. It was a social superpower and I started to harness it my sophomore year.

I was tired of being on the perimeter watching life from the sidelines. I craved belonging. I craved late nights of laughing and gossiping. I craved a place to sit in a crowded lunchroom, where people actually saved me a seat.

My experience at Peak High was completely different from what it had been at Peak Middle School. I went in determined to find my people, determined to find my place at the table.

That is how I met a small group of girls. I forced myself to be friendly, to brave the possibility of rejection. It felt as if I was on a mission with nothing left to lose. I always sat waiting for others to approach me, but somehow it never seemed to happen.

At the start of my sophomore year, I had a new mission: Operation Make Some Damn Friends. I was determined to be friendly and see where it got me.

"Hey," I said to a girl sitting alone in my English class. "Is anyone sitting there?" I pointed to the seat next to her.

She glanced over and said, "No, it's all yours." She smiled and made an exaggerated gesture to the empty seat.

She seemed friendly, so I did something I never even thought to do in the past and introduced myself. "I'm Natasha."

She smiled warmly. "I'm Deanna." She had a genuine feel to her. She had curly brown hair and a pale face that made her green eyes stand out. I instantly liked her.

I sat next to Deanna every day and we started to talk. My out-of-character move paid off in dividends. A few days later she asked, "Where do you eat lunch?"

I paused, and a flash of me walking alone popped in my head. After spending lunchtime in the bathroom last year, I was now spending lunchtime walking around campus. "Um... in the cafeteria," I lied.

"You should eat with us," she offered. "We eat outside."

I was instantly filled with excitement. The idea of not having to walk around killing time at lunch was priceless. I tried to act nonchalant. "Cool," I said, "I'd like that."

At lunch that day, I found Deanna and her two friends eating on the front steps of the school. "Hey, Natasha!" Deanna said, waving me over. I felt a knot in my stomach when I saw two girls sitting next to her. *What if they don't like me or, worse, think I'm invading their friend group?* "Jennifer and Sabrina, this is Natasha," she said, turning to the other girls sitting next to her. When they both smiled and said hi, the knot in my stomach cautiously untied. Jennifer had long brown hair and a friendly face.

"Where are you from?" Sabrina asked. She had short, jet-black hair and a no-nonsense air about her.

"Texas, but originally, I'm from Springfield. We moved back in February," I explained. They were surprised to hear I had been at their school the year before. I wanted to say, *Yeah, I was there. You probably didn't see me because I spent most of my free time hiding in the bathroom.*

That year we all hung out together. I had friends to hang out with at lunch, people to gossip with around my locker, and friendly faces in a sea full of students.

But just as happiness found me, my social anxiety did as well. Paro's faint whispers began to tickle my ear: *You don't fit in. They don't really like you.*

A picturesque town and a wonderful group of friends were no match for the deathly grip social anxiety had over me. It was a new chapter for Paro, a new move out of his ever-growing playbook. Operation: It's Not Good Enough with a side mission of They Don't Like You Anyway sprinkled in.

Social anxiety never leaves you alone. It makes you doubt your friendships. It makes you think the grass is always greener on the other side. It makes you feel unsettled. No longer could Paro ride the wave of my already rejection-filled environment, now he had to make waves of his own.

Towards the end of the year, we were sitting at lunch and they were all talking about a book they had read. This was a very cerebral group and even though Sabrina and Jennifer were in another socioeconomic bracket from Deanna and me, they all shared a quality of education of which I was deprived. Often, I was left out of these conversations, their vocabulary too expansive and their topics too complex for me to follow. During those times, I felt ignorant and out of place in the group. Paro would whisper, *You're not smart enough for this group.*

My social anxiety would always point out observations. *Sabrina and Jennifer are true best friends, you are just tagging along. Deanna really likes that other girl, Audrey, more than she likes you. I think they get together without you sometimes.*

And when those efforts didn't fully work, my social anxiety tried a new tactic. *This group is boring. You always get stuck with the boring, nerdy people. You are never the cool kid or in the popular group.* That was a tune that would eventually shake up my happy-ever-after throughout my life, and this was its debut.

* * *

The summer between my sophomore and junior year I went to

camp again, this time as a camp counselor at a different camp. Camp was always a booster shot for my self-esteem. I felt loved, wanted and accepted. It encouraged me to find my own unique voice and be myself. I came back bold and rejuvenated.

Having a solid group of friends that past year had been healing. I no longer lived in the shadows as a second-class citizen at school. I had a place to go at lunch and people to stand with during fire drills. I was part of a clique, part of a group. People knew where I belonged and who I belonged with, something I'd never had before.

In my life, I had spent so much energy trying to fit in. Fontaine was a disaster where I couldn't find my place amid the affluent popular kids and the tougher neighborhood kids. I couldn't get my footing at Ballard before I was swiftly taken away, and Peak Middle School had been a complete disaster.

Even among my newfound group, I felt like the odd one out. Regardless of socioeconomic status, they all had a vast vocabulary and a privileged education that I was only just starting to experience. I often felt bored during their conversations and found myself getting listless.

During my summer hiatuses I was able to shape shift into who I wanted to be with no risk of it impacting my social status (or lack thereof) at school. I was tired of trying to fit in. By now my summer's alter ego was starting to take form. I loved edgy, alternative music and I started to dabble in the punk scene. The idea of not trying to fit in anymore felt invigorating. The counterculture of not caring spoke to me like a long-lost friend offering me a way out. What if I stopped trying to be one of them? It wasn't as if I was doing a good job of it anyway. The music spoke to me, and the clothes said, "I'm not trying to be you." I fell in love and dived in head first.

When I returned home, my summer alter ego wanted to stick around. The color in my closet faded to black. I was going through a metamorphosis. There was liberation in this new style. It was an I-don't-want-to-be-like-you-anyway kind of style. It fed my self-esteem and quieted Paro. Paro could whisper all he wanted, but I didn't care. I didn't *want* them to like me. I didn't *want* to fit in. It was now my choice. There was power in feeling that I was rejecting them first, that I was choosing to be different rather than being labeled as different.

I also discovered that I may not have felt at home in my upscale neighborhood, but I was a short train ride to the coolest place on earth. A place where other people looked just like me and I finally felt at home. Every weekend I would ride the commuter train to New York City (NYC). I'd spend hours in the East Village going from one thrift store to another, searching for various shades of black to bring back to my reserved suburban town. Eventually my metamorphosis was complete, and I was unrecognizable to my old friends. If I was the odd one out before, I was a full-fledged black swan now. I don't think they knew what to make of me.

I no longer saw a hierarchy of popularity that I couldn't climb. I felt as if I belonged to a secret club that my small town didn't understand. I didn't want to climb the social ladder, in fact climbing had become unappetizing.

I had changed, and reverting back to who I used to be would never be an option. For once I had outsmarted Paro. I mocked him and beat him at his own game. *I don't want to be like them anyway! What do you have to say about that?!*

I didn't know it then, but I was about to jump ship; about to trade predictability and boredom for something with more flavor and inconsistency. I was a free agent and with my newfound confidence, I was subconsciously looking for a more exciting group to call home.

At school, I became more edgy and restless. I felt further and further disconnected from my friends. Their lives seemed so stable; their families so normal. Their conversations bored me and seemed so trivial.

That's when I met Rachel. Prior to meeting her I had developed a teen crush on the lead singer of Def Leppard. It was an obsessive crush only a teen could pull off. Posters on the wall kind of crush. It was odd because it didn't match my style or musical taste. I was mainly a Depeche Mode, Smiths kinda girl, but my teen hormones fixated on Joe Elliott.

In English class one day, we had to get into small groups to share our poems. I sat there doodling on my paper, zoning out, when a girl I barely paid attention to started reading her poem. I picked at my nails, bored, when something she said started to sound familiar. I felt as if I knew who she was writing about. I dropped my pen and started to listen.

As we went around the group sharing our obligatory commentary I went out on a limb and said, "I know this is going to sound totally weird, but it reminds me of the drummer of Def Leppard, the one who lost his arm."

I looked down after I said it, embarrassed I had revealed my knowledge about Def Leppard. But Rachel's eyes grew wide, and her mouth dropped, "Oh my God! How did you know? It *is* about him!"

I stopped picking at my nails and looked up to meet her gaze. I raised my eyebrows, "It is?"

Rachel's taste in drummers and her outward appearance didn't give you whiplash like mine did. She was a well-coordinated outfit. She was a meme of what an eighties head-banger should look like. She had black frizzy hair, sprayed to hang several inches above her head, acid wash jeans ripped and shredded in that rock-n-roll way, and a concert T-shirt to finish it off.

From then on, we became inseparable. She loved the drummer; I loved the lead singer. A friendship made in *Tiger Beat* teen heaven.

Rachel introduced me to her friends. Not exactly my cup of tea, but in a school with no black-clothed, Dr. Martens-wearing, Nine Inch Nails lovers, this was the next best thing. I was introduced to mini-Rachels. They all looked the same from the outside looking in. They were a headbanger, eighties heavy metal, acid-wash-wearing group. They weren't my people, far from it, but they were closer than my other friends.

My mutiny was swift and sudden. I started eating lunch with Rachel and her friends. I felt a swell of confidence start to build up. Her friends easily let me into the fold and the transition was smooth. I may have been the more seasoned, worldly one in my small innocent group, but I was a fish out of water in this one.

They drank, smoked and did drugs. They pushed the limits and snuck out. They lied to their parents and some traded sex for drugs. I left my world of *Barney & Friends* and traded it for *The Breakfast Club*. I was getting an education I wasn't sure I really wanted.

My old friends pretended not to notice. They never asked me to come back, never asked me why I had left.

Chapter 10
Now

Talking to Marty was like CPR to my lifeless soul and I continued to see her for a few more sessions. With her simple words she restored my determination to not let others tear me down. I would not let others define me. My wounds crusted over, and I picked at the scabs, anxious to rid myself of the memory.

At first I was angry. Angry with myself for giving my power away. Angry at how quickly I had lost all my footing with social anxiety. Upset at how easily Paro returned, waiting in the wings for his opportunity to suck up any light I had enjoyed.

But eventually my anger turned into fuel, fuel that aggressively dared anyone to try and knock me down. I no longer cared about what anyone thought. I no longer cared about how I was viewed. I no longer cared if I belonged.

It is amazing how freeing it is to not care. It was a freedom that even at the peak of my social anxiety recovery, I had not fully achieved. Like a burn that needed to be painfully scraped off in order to heal, I had to be completely broken in order to be set free.

As I got the kids in the car I thought how easy drop-offs had become. I no longer scanned each car for a judging scowl. I no longer worried that people were talking about me. If they were, let them. I simply didn't care. Why had I ever?

Alex was in a grumpy mood. Her anxiety had been growing, the apple not falling far from the genetic tree. She didn't want to go to school. Her stomach was in knots, and she was begging to stay home.

We did our usual dance. She told me her fears and I coached her through. "But what if I throw up, Mom?" she asked, her small frame hunched over. "No one will be my friend," she pleaded. A cocktail of emetophobia (the fear of throwing up) and social anxiety was destroying her first grade year.

"Then what do you need to tell yourself?" I prompted, my words familiar to her ears. She sat for a minute and then whispered, "Then they aren't nice people anyway and who needs friends like that."

"Exactly," I said, smiling and giving her a tight hug. She finished tying her shoe and grabbed her backpack. We were going to be late for school.

As we pulled up to the school it looked like a ghost town. It was hard to believe that just ten minutes before the parking lot had been buzzing with parents and hurried kids.

We followed another car into the drop-off lane. We were the only two cars running late that morning. There were strict rules in the drop-off lane. Stay to the right. Only let your child out on the blue line. Pull all the way up.

These rules were emailed to us and plastered on a rickety board with a handwritten reminder in case you forgot. And just for good measure, the school invested in a yellow gate, blocking the other lane, making it impossible for anyone to drive outside the single-file drop-off lane and break the rules.

As the other car pulled in front of the school, it abruptly stopped parallel to the yellow gate, blocking the other lane and boxing me in. My kids grabbed their backpacks, said their I love yous, and headed to the office to sign in. As they slammed the door and rushed inside, I saw the dad of the other car get out and leave. He wore saggy sweatpants, and his disheveled hair flew in every direction.

I looked behind me. There were no other cars in sight. I was trapped. My jaw tightened as I realized I was now forced to wait for him to return. It seemed purposeful. If he had pulled up even a few more feet I would have been able to swerve around him and get out of the pick-up lane.

The old me would have sat back and waited for him to finish going to the office and eventually come back.

But this wasn't the old me. This was the fuel-injected Natasha Version 2.0. She didn't sit around and not advocate for herself. Before I could even contemplate my next step, I found myself lightly tapping on my horn. I was in my own version of sweats and had no inclination to actually get out of my car. The man turned to me, his face already in a scowl. I smiled and mouthed the words, "Can you move up, please?" as I gestured with my hands to show I was boxed in.

"Fuck you!" he spewed, his voice shaking my closed windows. He spat on the concrete and added, "Deal with it," and then continued walking towards the office.

My hands started to shake as I tightened my grip on the

steering wheel. I was filled with a mixture of rage and nervous adrenaline. "Are you kidding me?" I screamed through the closed windows.

I saw myself put the car in reverse and jam on the gas, hitting his car repeatedly. It felt good. It took all my control to not really do it. I felt so much rage in that moment. It was the culmination of everything I had been feeling for weeks. Every ounce of my body wanted to slam on the gas. I took a deep breath and tried to loosen the grip on the wheel. Going to jail wasn't part of my plan for the day.

I then thought to myself, *Am I giving my power away?* Hadn't I just committed to not let anyone tear me down? He was obviously having a bad day, maybe a bad life. *Should I allow him to ruin my day? Should I allow him the satisfaction of spewing his darkness on my morning?*

No. I took some deep breaths, trying to move the cortisol and adrenaline out of my body. I counted. I became my own therapist. *This isn't about me. This guy doesn't even know me. This is about him needing to exert power. That's about him and his story, not about me and mine.*

My breathing started to return to normal. My hands started to loosen their grip. I fantasized about what kind of life he must be living to crave such a cruel exchange with a stranger.

A woman drove up behind me, more hurried than I was ten minutes ago. I stared at her in the rear-view mirror. I thought, *It's not me, lady.* I could tell she was growing annoyed. She pulled her car in reverse and moved alongside me, the yellow gate blocking her freedom. Welcome to the club.

She hadn't even hesitated to move past me before abruptly

being stopped by the yellow gate. I thought, that's what it must be like to not live with social anxiety. No hesitation at all in her actions.

The man returned, a smirk on his beaten-down face, a small win to lighten his misery. He looked at both of our cars trapped behind him with what seemed to be a sense of accomplishment. He slowed his stride, seemingly reveling in his power. I took another deep breath and whispered to myself, *I will not give you the power to ruin my day.*

Finally, we were freed from the parking lot and his ego trip. I watched in dismay as I followed the miserable man back to my subdivision, turn for turn. *Another friendly neighbor to look out for*, I thought. *Now there are at least two.*

I got back home and grabbed my work bag and poured myself another cup of coffee. It was going to be a long day of therapy sessions and I needed the extra boost. I paused and checked in with myself to see if there was any emotional residue from what had just happened. I could normally stew on something like this for days, if not weeks. I was pleasantly surprised to find that I had truly let it go. I legitimately did not care. I had no anger, no embarrassment, no victim mentality. I was just moving on.

Good, I thought. *It's about time.*

* * *

I sipped my coffee and looked at my schedule. It was a full day, but I needed to make room for Miss 18. I was determined to continue making this a priority.

I had an hour before my first appointment, plenty of time to visit with my old self. I wondered how long I would do this? Until time intersected and brought me to the present? I guess we would have to see.

I was less concerned about meeting Miss 18 than I was about the other younger versions of myself. She was less wounded or more hardened, it was hard to say which. I opened the door and peered out. She sat up tall in the chair, her arms folded over herself protectively. Her large black sweater swallowed her up and hid any discomfort. Her thin legs were wrapped in black tights and her maroon Docs anchored her to the floor. I smiled and gestured for her to come in.

"Hi," she said, a warmth to her voice that caught me off guard.

"Hey," I said, putting my hands in my back pockets and rocking back and forth as she walked past me.

I motioned for her to sit where all her previous selves had sat.

"How's it going?" I said, wishing it was easier to start these sessions.

"Good," she said, "I'm excited to be going off to college soon."

"Yes, that will be so good. How was high school?" She stared down at her black nails. I already knew how she was feeling. She had been injected with turbo level self-confidence at the end of her sophomore year. It had felt exhilarating, but now she questioned if she had made the right choice to leave her more stable group of friends.

As she was preparing to go off to college, her friends were still doing drugs and stuck in the past. She realized that her only true friend in that group was Rachel. No one else asked to keep in touch or even cared what she was doing after high school.

"It was okay, I guess. I never really felt like I fitted in there," she said, opening up more than I expected. She paused for a second, staring past me. "Honestly, I probably shouldn't have left my first group of friends. They really weren't that bad."

I was surprised by her insight. "So why didn't you go back to them? Leave the people you were hanging with?"

She repositioned herself and bit her lower lip, "I guess it was just too late. I had already moved on. They had already moved on. I don't think they even cared or wanted me back."

She paused to pick some invisible lint off her pants and then continued.

"Living in that town was like being an exchange student for four years. I never felt that I really belonged there. I was always waiting to go back home, only I had no home. I had no other place where I belonged."

I sat silently, a pain developing in my chest. I remembered those feelings as if it were yesterday. I felt like an observer, never a participant. Even after years passed and I would go back to visit, I always felt as if I was in someone else's hometown, not mine.

"What you might come to realize as time passes," I began, choosing my words carefully, "is that you won't *ever* feel that you are home, anywhere. That a part of you will always feel as if you are the guest or, worse, the imposter. But, in reality, that isn't the case. It's your perception that makes it so." I scanned her face to see a reaction.

She stared at my bookshelf, her mind seemingly a hundred miles away. Then she looked back at me and said, "Really? I hope that isn't the case." Perhaps the pain of that revelation was too deep to consider.

She exhaled and then said, "I think it was just because I was the new kid in a small town. Everyone knew each other already."

"Yes, you'll have reasons," I said gently. "You'll always have reasons why you felt like the outsider. You will feed yourself excuses, which allow you to hide the real reason you'll never feel as if you belong." My words had a sting, but my voice was soft.

Her eyebrows came together, and she shrugged. "I don't get it. What's the real reason?" I thought I could see a mixture of hurt and confusion on her face.

I took a breath and then said, "You have social anxiety. Social anxiety will always tell you that you don't fit in. It will feed you lies about how you don't belong. It will sell you a story so subtle that you won't even notice that it's not the truth."

A small smile started to peek through her confusion, and her posture relaxed. "Oh...you think this is because of social anxiety? No, I don't have anxiety." She waved her hand in the air defensively, as if she was swatting an annoying fly away.

"Yes, that's the problem with that form of anxiety," I insisted. "It is so good, you don't even realize it's there." I was hoping to open her eyes even just a little bit.

A quick frown flashed across her face before her smile returned. "I can get anxious about my safety or scared when I'm home alone. I even get nervous sometimes at night when the house is dark. But socially? No, that doesn't make me anxious. I definitely don't have social anxiety." I realized that this diagnosis might be insulting to her, especially since she'd made progress.

I tried to explain it again, this time more clearly. "Most people think social anxiety is about being shy or being an introvert, but it's not. It's about the fear of rejection. It's about the fear of being criticized or judged. It's about feeling so self-conscious, you feel like you are on stage and a spotlight is following you no matter where you go. It's about worrying what others think so deeply that it can completely shut you down," I finished my rambling and got off my soapbox.

I could tell I had hit a nerve. Behind her flat expression, a flicker in her eyes started to stir. I knew my words were resonating with her and she knew I was right. "I didn't realize social anxiety was all of that," she said, her voice softer and less sure.

We talked about her long history of worrying that she didn't fit in. We talked about Fontaine, Ballard, and all the other places where she felt she failed. We talked about her bumpy start in Peak and how she was able to find herself in the last couple of years of high school.

We wrapped up our session. She had a whole new chapter to go and live out—a chapter that would be exhilarating and chaotic, all at the same time.

I walked her to the door. She turned to me and said, "Thanks for taking the time to talk to me. It's good you are doing this. I think it will really help you."

I was taken aback by her sudden motherly tone. I stammered and finally said, "Yes, I hope it will." The sudden change in roles felt awkward and comforting all at the same time.

Chapter 11
Then
Anderson Hill Road

I was finally free. But I wasn't the only one who seemed to desire freedom. My dad's bipolar disorder had crippled him and he was more unpredictable and infantile in his mannerisms. He would whisper in conspiratorial tones how he was making plans to leave my mom.

We both packed our bags. I went to college and my dad went to live at his work. He slept in his lab and his boss was none the wiser. It was strange times. He filed for divorce, and I filed for financial aid. We both got what we wanted.

My mom drove me the hour away to my new campus. I felt jittery and anxious the whole way up. *What if I don't make friends up there? This could be a whole new chapter, or it could be further confirmation that I repel people.*

I didn't know a soul. I walked into my new dorm room and my roommate greeted me with a huge smile. She bounced off her bed and said, "Hey! You must be Natasha!" pulling me into a bear hug. She smelled of cigarettes, patchouli and acceptance. I instantly liked her.

Melody had long, jet-black hair, red lips and combat boots

that spoke almost as loudly as she did. She was the life of the party and full of love. She was a perfect first roommate.

For the first few days of school we roamed the campus together foraging for our new group of friends. It was exhilarating to be enveloped by her confidence; it was contagious.

On one of the first nights we gathered like a swarm of bees by a Henry Moore sculpture. A buzz was in the air, and you could feel all the infinite social possibilities. A voice in the dark shouted, "We should create nicknames for ourselves." People started to nod.

"Yeah, what do you want to be called?" Everyone threw out names for each other.

As I saw the enthusiasm build, it made me wonder if these people were equally desperate to erase who they had been? The answer would come a few months later as I scrolled through a photo album belonging to my then blue-haired boyfriend. He was the only one to keep his new name from that night, going from Ben to Sheker.

I did a double-take as I stared at a picture of him and his friends from high school. In the picture, Ben had brown hair and glasses and stood awkwardly next to his equally geeky friends. He caught me looking at it and pounced off his bed. "Give that to me." He grabbed the album and slammed it shut. I thought I saw fear dance across his face. Maybe fear of being found out? Fear that the facade of his bad boy punk exterior would all come crumbling down?

I wanted to tell him not to worry. That he was not alone. That we were all hiding something, but to do so would be to reveal my own tightly worn mask.

* * *

The rest of my first year was a blur. I was intoxicated with the idea of belonging and I interjected myself into several tightly knit groups to soak up the love.

I hopped from group to group, party to party, boyfriend to boyfriend. Like an excited butterfly, I didn't know where to land. I fluttered around and lost my footing. I belonged everywhere and nowhere at the same time.

While people were solidifying their friendships, I was being left behind. Many groups welcomed me in, but none of them felt like home anymore. They were spending all their time laughing and joking together, while I was becoming a periodic visitor. It happened so subtly I didn't realize what I was doing until it was too late.

I once again had nowhere to call home. This time I could firmly blame myself. Like a child given a huge piece of cake, I indulged myself, determined to eat the whole thing in one sitting. Now I was left with nothing to show for it except indigestion.

Paro tried to get in on the misery, but I firmly shut him down and took responsibility. No, this wasn't about me repelling people. No, this wasn't about me not fitting in. This time it was about me having too big a feast.

As the school year ended, I wasn't sure what to do or where to go. My mom had moved into a small two-bedroom apartment on Anderson Hill Road, with just enough room for her and Allison. My dad had wooed a colleague, and they were living in her apartment.

I had nowhere to call home, literally this time. So, with nowhere really to go, I went to live with my aunt and uncle and my cousin Joel back in Brooklyn. Joel was also on summer break from college, and we had reconnected. He and I decided that it might be easy to get a job working at one of the big clubs in the city.

We took the subway into NYC and found the dirty black door behind the club. We both looked at each other and shrugged. Joel looked at his scribbled instructions again. "It says knock on the black door." We knocked on the door and a few minutes later a large bald man in a muscle shirt answered. He grunted a few words and pointed us to the stairs. Fifteen minutes later we were officially employees of one of the coolest clubs in NYC.

Joel and I took the subway from Brooklyn for the next few nights. The job was less than glamorous. Picking up glasses and cleaning up barf, wasn't exactly what I had pictured. The club scene was pretty gross when you had a front-row seat to it all. My nights consisted mostly of watching random people have sex in the seats above the dance floor as the bouncers laughed and put a spotlight on them. My nose burned with the smell of alcohol, vomit and cologne. It was all a bit too much.

About five days into the job, I had a shift alone. I was nervous to take the subway back in the middle of the night, so my aunt and uncle loaned me their car.

The music's bass pounded through my body as I grabbed glasses on the dance floor. I headed up to the second floor and dumped the glasses in the kitchen and headed back out. It seemed never ending. I leaned over the balcony to take a break. It was interesting to watch some people dance. There was a girl who was drawing a small crowd. She must have been a professional dancer. I had seen her a few nights before. Her dancing seemed choreographed as she rhythmically moved her body perfectly to the music. *God, I wish I had that kind of talent.*

I was so enamored with her skill that I barely saw the fight break out until two men nearly fell right into her. My heart stopped and my skin prickled.

The fight spread like wildfire, a small spark leading to big flames. Within seconds everyone on the entire floor was throwing punches instead of dance moves. I stood by the rail, my heart pounding in my chest, my feet two blocks of cement. Bouncers, like angry wasps, swarmed the floor trying to separate the groups. The music thudded rhythmically in the background.

I stood with my bird's-eye view, watching this unfold, my eyes wide, my body five hundred pounds of sand. And then I heard a loud bang as everyone on the dance floor scattered. At first my brain didn't register what my ears were hearing. I leaned over the balcony to get a better view.

Bang! Another shot. This time I saw a guy fall, liquid oozing beneath him. Something deep inside me started to whisper, and after the third shot it started to scream...*RUN!*

I jolted back from the balcony, breaking free from my paralysis, and took in the scene. People were running everywhere. Furniture was turned upside down and people were hiding underneath it. I ran to the back stairwell, taking the stairs two at a time, a crowd of screaming people running behind me. I got to the bottom floor and one of the managers motioned for employees to go left. I ran in that direction. More gunfire came from upstairs.

"This isn't safe, let's go in here," he said, shooing us into another room and quickly closing the door. I took in my surroundings. We were in a long hallway and on one side there was what looked like a jail. The room to the side was covered with bars and could only be accessed through a wrought iron gate. The manager opened the gate with a key. "Come in here!" he motioned. Girls dressed in scantily clad clothes piled in. I followed behind them.

"No," he said holding his hand up to me, "Only cocktail waitresses who are carrying money. The rest of you stay out there." I stood there, my mind swirling, trying to make sense of what was happening. It was then that I saw the large safes behind the bars and the dumbwaiter that went from the dance floor down to the safes.

There was plenty of room in there for all of us, but we were not as valuable as the money or the cocktail waitresses. We lined up and sat against the wall. I sat at the back of the hall, directly facing the front door. It occurred to me then that out of the 20 people huddled in the hallway, I had the worst seat in the house. My mind flashed to what-if scenes. I imagined a gunman running down the stairs, trying the locked door, pulling back his semi-automatic and spraying bullets through the door. I saw myself slump over, my life pouring out of me.

The manager stood on the dumbwaiter and poked his head on to the dance floor.

"They're still up there," he whispered.

It sounded like a herd of elephants above. Screams and

shots could be heard echoing throughout the building. *What a stupid way to die*, I thought. I had positioned myself in the worst possible place. I was sitting right next to the money. And not only that, I was sitting in the line of fire if anyone tried to get in.

What was I doing? I thought back to what had just happened. I replayed running down the stairs, seeing the manager motion for us to go left. Why hadn't I gone right? I rewound the scene in my head and saw two large doors open on to the street. People were running in that direction. Why had I listened to the manager and gone away from a simple escape?

I was blindly following directions, still acting like an employee. And now I found myself sitting in a room, in the most precarious spot of them all, still not finding my voice. I resigned to the fact that I might get shot. I felt trapped. I held my knees to my chest and felt the steady tremor of my body shaking.

The manager, hovering between floors, leaned down from the dumbwaiter and whispered, "The cops are on the way."

I held my knees tighter and reassured myself that the shooting wasn't a robbery, probably just a fight. I strained my ears to listen for sirens. It felt like an eternity, but, eventually, I could hear them in the distance.

As soon as the police came and cleared the building, the body tremors stopped and I tensed with rage. I was angry at the manager who placed more value on money than human lives. I was angry at myself for being a sheep who followed the herd to the slaughter. I vowed to myself that I would never go back to that place. It had stepped on my worth and I wouldn't let it happen again.

But a nagging feeling remained. Why didn't I just run out

of the building? The doors were wide open. And when I was put in a dangerous spot, why didn't I just get up and leave or change seats?

It's funny what we do in crisis situations. It was like the time when, so worried about what people might think, I didn't call out for help as my ankle was slowly breaking in the rapids.

It had felt too overwhelming to go against what the manager said. It felt too embarrassing to get up and walk out and disregard what I was told to do, even when it put me in harm's way. I promised to never be that blind again. I would never sacrifice my emotional or physical well-being for the sake of others. I would never feel so small and inconsequential that I took no action to keep myself safe. My worth and value had to come before anything else. If I didn't protect myself, no one else would.

Chapter 12
Then

Green Village Road

I returned to my sophomore year of college with zero excitement. I was placed in an on-campus apartment full of strangers. It wasn't ideal. I spent the semester watching friendships fade and my place at college grow smaller and smaller. The worst part was that I blamed myself. I felt as if I had been given high-quality clay to build some beautiful friendships and instead I overworked the clay until it couldn't even keep its form.

By the time sophomore year ended and the summer rolled around, I had lost all my sparkle for the place. I reluctantly secured my spot in the same apartment for the following year and took off to work as a counselor at a sleepaway camp with Jake and Joel.

At camp, I instantly felt like a fish out of water. I had flashbacks of the cliquey girls from my childhood. I looked at their feet and every single girl was sporting the same boots. I had not got the memo. They had a style that came from a rule book I had never read. My partially shaved jet-black hair and combat boots had no place in their universe and they made sure to let me know that.

The staff were all moving into their cabins. The campers were going to arrive the following week and we'd be preparing the camp until then. As I was walking back to get the last of my stuff, the director motioned for me to come over. He led me over by the trees, out of earshot of everyone else. He quietly said, "We are going to have to ask you to move to another cabin."

My eyebrows squished together in confusion, "Wait, but why? I've just unpacked most of my things?"

He kicked the dirt around, his bald head starting to perspire, and then looked up. "Some girls have been complaining," he paused, seemingly unsure of how to finish his sentence. "They're worried you might steal their stuff."

My eyes widened and I shook my head, "What? Are you kidding me? That's ridiculous. Why would they say that?"

His eyes darted around. "I don't know, but we don't want any problems. Just get your stuff and move to cabin 1A." He pointed to the cabin behind us.

I just stood there. I would no longer be anyone's punching bag and I didn't appreciate being accused of something I would never think to do. "You know, they are making that up because they want to be together, right?" I challenged. I was tired of being pushed around. I wasn't the same girl that got bulldozed in middle school.

His tone got firmer, "Just do it." And before I could argue any further he walked away.

I swallowed hard.

* * *

The next day, we were assigned tasks around camp to get it prepared for the campers. The camp cut corners in every way possible. They had the camp counselors paint and repair the cabins.

We were placed in groups. I was feeling as if I was back in junior high again. Jake and Joel were already making friends and ignoring me. It felt like deja vu. Why did they always fit in, and I was the outcast? Only this time I didn't feel insecure, I felt angry. I was tired of being trampled on and made to feel insignificant. I was angry with the whole camp. I was angry with the snobby girls who made me repack so they could be together. I was angry with the director who was complicit in their judgmental behavior. I was angry with Jake and Joel who once again left me out without even realizing it.

In the sea of staff, I heard several people with English accents. The camp was part of an exchange program. In an effort to cut even more corners, many of the staff were brought in as foreign exchange students whose payment consisted solely of room and board.

We were assigned to repaint all of the picnic tables around camp. It was a lofty assignment that would take us days to complete. I surveyed the group to see who, if anyone, I could talk to for the next few days. I saw a quiet gangly guy with short brown hair sitting on a bench. I thought I had heard him speak with a British accent.

I sat next to him on the bench and turned to him, "Hey, are you British?"

"Yeah," he said giving me a crooked smile with a mouth of equally crooked teeth. "Where are you from?"

For the next few hours he was my source of entertainment. I was stuck at this camp with a group of unapproachable girls, but I was determined to make the best of it.

I kept staring at him trying to decide if he was cute or not. His accent swayed me to do a virtual swipe right in my head. "Come sit up in the front with me," I said, opening the passenger side of the beat-up truck we had been riding in.

His name was Ricky, and he was from England. We spent the rest of the day together, our fate sealed in spattered paint and overalls. From then on, we were inseparable. I was in love with being loved. It felt good to be wanted. It felt good to not be alone. Jake and Joel could ignore me. The mean girls could glare. None of it mattered anymore. I had somewhere to be and *someone* to be with.

Everyone in camp started to pair up one by one. Singles became doubles wherever you looked. Jake and I compared notes. He had found himself his own British accent.

Periodically I would panic and wonder if I was even attracted to Ricky. Sometimes I would see him walking towards me and I'd feel a wave of nausea instead of attraction. I would feel trapped and would wonder if I should break up with him. It was nice to feel wanted and loved, but was I forcing it? I would bounce from a feeling of disgust to a feeling of belonging. I was way behind my peers when it came to relationships. I had experienced a small handful of boyfriends at college, but no relationship lasted more than a few months. It felt good to have a place I belonged.

* * *

Eventually, I let go of the nagging feeling Ricky was the wrong person for me and just focused on the fun a summer fling had to offer. But the camp was poorly run and I continued to bump heads with the camp director. Eventually I felt I just had to quit.

I searched for Ricky near his bunk and let him know what was happening.

"You can't quit. What about me?" he said, a look of hurt and confusion on his face.

"I'm sorry, but I can't stomach this place any longer. You can come with me if you want. I'm sure my mom would let you stay at her house?" I offered.

But Ricky was under contractual obligation to stay a little bit longer to work off his room and board.

Ricky would later tell me that Jake and Joel called a staff meeting that night. A meeting where they stood up for me and called out the director for all his unprofessional behavior. He said it was like a scene in a movie and that he wished I could have seen it. I wish I had been there too. It would have been so healing to hear that they actually cared.

Jake and Joel quit soon after and they came back to my mom's house with Ricky and Mary, my brother's new girlfriend, in tow. In an attempt to salvage the summer, we scraped up enough money to take a road trip from New Jersey to Florida for a $99 three-day cruise in the Bahamas. As the trip progressed, I realized I truly didn't want to be with Ricky.

On the beaches of Florida, I took a stab at pulling off the Band-Aid. I moved the sand around my feet as we stood facing the ocean. "I don't think this is working out," I started, putting my hands in my pockets. "When you go back to England I want to just be friends. I think you should date other people." I stared ahead, not wanting to see his reaction.

He moved closer. "No, I won't do that. You can date other people, but I won't see anyone but you."

A pit grew at the bottom of my stomach. I wanted this to be easy. This talk wasn't going the way I wanted it to go. I took my hands out of my pockets and turned fully towards him. "No, you don't understand," I tried again, looking directly at him. "I want you to see other people. I don't think we should stay together."

He shook his head no. He wasn't budging. I don't know why I felt that I needed his approval. I should have realized I could break up whether he agreed or not. But there I was trying to get him to allow me to end our relationship. When he said no, I accepted defeat.

In the future, I would replay that moment and wonder why I had accepted his no. Why I had allowed him to talk me back into a relationship I wanted no part in. I would wonder how life would have turned out if I had followed what I wanted instead of what someone else wanted. I would wonder why I always put other people's needs first, always ahead of my own. But this is an issue I wouldn't start exploring until I reached my forties.

The Florida trip continued and, unfortunately, so did our relationship. It was as if the conversation never happened. Instead of fighting for what I wanted, I convinced myself that perhaps being together was what we *both* wanted.

When the summer ended, Ricky went back to England, and I went back to college. The plan was for us to keep a long-distance relationship while I finished my two remaining years of college.

When I arrived back at my college apartment I felt miserable. I had four roommates who were practically strangers. My friendships on campus had shriveled up and I didn't feel close to anyone. The idea of two more years there made my stomach churn.

I called my mom and told her I needed to take the semester off. My parents had got back together, and the only silver lining was that they had recently moved into a new place and had room for one more. I was living at their apartment by the following week.

Living at home was like being stuck in a can of molasses. I had nothing to do and nowhere to be. Time was in slow motion. Eventually I got a job at a bagel shop. Prior to that I had successfully avoided any job that required me to 1) work with the public or 2) operate a cash register, as both gave me heart palpitations.

I learned to survive my new job and in my oodles of spare time, I wrote to Ricky. The old cliche, *absence makes the heart grow fonder*, was the relationship's saving grace and my long-term downfall. I romanticized his absence. By the time Ricky came back to the States I had created a love story that was pure fiction. I had fallen in love with the idea of being loved once again.

When I visited him in England all the pent-up excitement and romanticism I had created would come crashing down. Panic would bubble up and I would feel trapped and claustrophobic. I would spend half the trip mentally anguishing over if he was the right person for me and the second half thinking about how to break up. Sadly, as soon as I built up the courage to break up, I would be on my way back home, only to start the whole cycle again.

It felt good to be loved. It felt good to be someone's everything. I never had that before and I wanted to bottle up the feeling of belonging forever. Perhaps that is why I said yes when Ricky proposed to me during his next visit.

My mom was concerned. She knew I had mixed feelings. As we sat around the kitchen table, she asked, "Are you sure that's what you want?" Worry was etched on her forehead.

I was annoyed that she knew me so well. I didn't want anyone to question me, I was already too unsure myself. I put my hand nervously to my neck, "I think so."

And that was that. We sublet an apartment on Green Village Road, as I followed in my mom's footsteps and married a man from another country before I was even legally able to drink. Both of us trapped. Both of us underwhelmed by our choice but enticed by the feeling of love. Ugly history has a way of repeating itself.

Chapter 13
Now

I read the email again. A little voice piped in, "Can you go, Mommy? I really want you to go with me." I looked at my little girl, her puppy dog eyes staring up at me waiting for a response.

My old anxious self wouldn't have even thought twice. I didn't *do* field trips. I would have made an excuse and convinced myself it was the truth. Neither of us would have been the wiser. But I refused to let Paro tighten his grip on me any longer. I knew how devastating it could be when I let him back in.

"Sure, honey, I'd love to go to the butterfly museum," I lied, feeling a twinge of nausea. "It will be fun," I lied again, this time more for my benefit than for hers.

Before I could change my mind, I hit reply to the email and quickly typed, "I'd love to go!"

This would be a big test. It would be putting Paro in a position where he has always had the upper hand. This was his playground and I had just invited him to play in it. But I knew I needed to practice what I preached. I spent my days helping kids with anxiety and OCD face their fears. I taught parents online how to motivate their kids to do just this, and now I needed to do it for myself.

The morning of the field trip, Alex was nervous. "I'm scared," she said as she grabbed her lunch and put it in her backpack. Her Paro Junior was just starting to get wings. It made my heart hurt that she had to deal with a similar beast. I moved swiftly into our new routine, "What are you the most scared about?"

She bit at her nail as she sat at the kitchen counter. "What if I feel sick? What if I have to go to the bathroom?" She opened her fidget basket and grabbed a squishy.

It sounded familiar. She was listing her anxiety's favorite playlist of issues. We had been through this dance so many times. I made my next move. "What can you tell yourself? What's your green thought?" She seemed to like it when we did this. We called her anxious thoughts red thoughts and her positive thoughts green thoughts. She usually calmed down afterwards.

She squeezed the watermelon squishy and said, "Well, my green thought is that I always feel like this when I am going somewhere new and I never get sick," and then she quickly added, "but, even if I do, it will be okay. Everyone throws up once in a while." She stared at me for a response.

"Good! Exactly. How about the bathroom fear?" I asked, wanting to fully pull out any Paro Junior weeds that were waiting to sprout.

"Well, I know I can hold it for hours, so no matter what I don't have to worry." The lines on her forehead smoothed out and the color started coming back into her cheeks.

"Exactly!" I said, proud of her ability to walk herself through her fears at only six. I didn't learn how to walk through my anxieties until I was in my forties. I thought about what life would have been like if my anxiety had even been acknowledged, let alone worked on.

I grabbed her little hand in mine. "It will be fun!" I said, this time more for her than for me. "We get to spend the day together and that is worth it all."

A few hours after dropping her off I pulled into the parking lot. I hadn't been one of the parents chosen to ride the bus, thank goodness. I saw a group of parents gathering in front of the museum. They were huddled in a few small circles.

I had flashbacks of driving up to Fontaine and feeling overwhelmed by the groups of students in their tightly formed circles reminding me I didn't belong.

I loosened my grip on the steering wheel and gave myself green thoughts. *You are here to spend time with Alex. Don't make this about you. Besides, who cares what people think. Right?*

But Paro didn't lose an opportunity to pounce. *This is going to be so uncomfortable. Maybe you should just wait until the buses get here so you can be with Alex. That way you don't have to stand there alone and feel like a loser when no one talks to you?*

No! I snapped back. *Avoidance is what feeds you and keeps you growing. I'm done growing you. In fact, I am getting out of this car right now to make sure I am out there before she arrives. And I think I'll take a seat right over there in the middle of all those parents. That will make you squirm, won't it, Paro?*

I got out of the car and walked towards the group. There were no friendly waves or nods of recognition. I had isolated myself long ago. There had been no small talk at birthday parties. There had been no volunteering in the classroom to develop lifelong friendships with the other moms. No one knew me and I didn't know them.

I found a seat in the sun. It was a beautiful Arizona day, blue skies and a nice breeze. I watched people coming and going. It was a busy day for field trips, I counted at least three other schools as I sat on the bench.

I watched as two little kids tried to climb up the sculpture in front of me. One had her tongue out, sheer determination all over her face. Eventually, the little girl grabbed the hand of her friend and strained to pull her up. She looked over at me with a big smile. I smiled back and put my hands together, silently clapping for her accomplishment. She took a bow to her audience of one. I felt as if I repelled adults and was the Pied Piper to kids, and there was no in-between.

With a smile still on my face, I noticed that something was off. My body felt normal. No tingles, no clammy hands, no upset stomach. I realized that I wasn't nervous. I didn't feel conspicuous at all. I wasn't trying to *look* comfortable; I *was* comfortable. It was so subtle that I almost missed it. The magnitude of this epiphany almost brought me to tears. I was sitting alone in a sea full of cliques and for the first time in my life, I didn't care. I did not survey the crowd to see who was staring at me. I did not create dialogue in my head convincing me I was the topic of all conversations. I did not tell myself to look busy and then anxiously grab my phone. I did none of those things. Not because I was distracted by the cute kids on the sculpture, but because I truly did not care. I did not care what they thought. I was not interested in a debate with Paro. It was a debate I no longer cared to argue. If they didn't like me, they didn't like me. The whole thing had lost its allure.

The buses arrived and we went in. We spent the day

watching the metamorphosis of the butterfly. We watched the stages of transformation as the butterfly cocooned itself so tight that it might have felt trapped and alone. All the while it was transforming and working towards a new life that would be more freeing than anything else it had ever known before.

* * *

Later that day I headed to my office for a few evening sessions. As I walked up the stairs to my building I felt lighter. Today had been a big victory against Paro. I had put myself in the lion's den and I had come out unscathed. It gave me hope for the future and renewed my faith in myself.

I had purposely carved out some time before my first appointment. These sessions with my younger self had become a priority in my healing. I no longer questioned how long I should be meeting with myself. I decided I would do it until I caught up with who I am. I had a lot of healing to do along the way.

Still feeling light from the day's events, I opened the door to greet Miss 23. I was more bubbly than normal. "Well, hello there," I said, greeting my younger self sitting on the chair in the hall.

She was petite and thin, wearing a gray miniskirt and a black turtleneck. Her black hair was worn in a short, shaggy pixie cut. When she saw me coming out, she nervously tucked her hair behind one ear. "Hi," she said as she got up and moved towards my office.

It felt weird talking to the adult version of me. In previous sessions I had felt maternal, wanting to protect my inner child from the pain that she had experienced. But this was different, my maternal oozing had dried up and I was left with a more sisterly bond with Miss 23.

"So, where should we start?" I asked her, not feeling the burden of having to carry the conversation with this older self.

She shrugged one shoulder. "I'm not sure. I think things are going pretty well right now."

I noticed how she sat up straighter and her gaze was more direct than previous versions of her. "Okay, let's start with what life is like right now," I suggested, knowing there were many areas to focus on.

"Well, I work in New York City for this advertising company. I commute back and forth. Ricky and I live in an apartment near the train station in a small town in New Jersey. We don't have a car, so luckily we can walk to everything."

I remembered those times. The most exciting thing we did was eat out at the local Mexican restaurant or buy one item at the thrift store down the street. Money was tight.

"How's it going with Ricky?" I remembered how trapped and frustrated I felt at the time.

She stalled. She wasn't used to admitting she had made a big mistake. She had too much pride. "Uh, it's fine," she said, lacing her hands tightly together. "Although we are really complete opposites."

"In what way?" I prompted, more for her to see than for me.

She unlaced her hands, tucking one arm under the other, while pulling the skin at her neck. "He talks to everyone. I think I don't belong anywhere, and he thinks he belongs everywhere, even when he doesn't. Honestly, he can be embarrassing. The things he says to people..." she scrunched her face up in disgust. "It's..." she looked up, searching for the right words. "Uncomfortable," she finally said, bringing her hands tightly together again.

I knew exactly what she meant. I also knew she had to handle the brunt of the household responsibilities.

I switched topics, not wanting to push her too far, too soon. "How's work going? Do you like being in advertising?"

She laughed dryly and said, "I'm hardly in advertising. Being an assistant is like being a second-class citizen there. It's like being invited to a party, but you are there to serve the guests. I am invisible to them; that is, unless someone needs me." She straightened her skirt and scooted back in her seat, staring at the floor.

I remembered that feeling of being invisible. It was torture. "Unfortunately, that job and the ones that will come after it really hurt your confidence," I warned. "You already feel as if you don't fit in, and these jobs do nothing but reconfirm that."

She looked up and nodded, "Yeah, it's true. I feel like a nobody there."

"But here's the thing," I said, leaning closer to her, "You settle. You have settled for a marriage that brings you more frustration than joy because you don't think you are lovable. When you did that you put your career goals on hold because now you can't afford graduate school. You are in a job you never wanted, and your life is stuck in a holding pattern." I could feel my own frustration coming back as I talked.

I think I was overwhelming her. She put her hands up in defeat. "It's not that bad really. It'll be okay. I'm going to save up and go to graduate school in a few years. And as far as love goes, I keep telling myself maybe I'll find true love in my next life," she chuckled, but I knew there was some truth to what she was saying.

"Why not this life?" I challenged. "You are worthy right now, in this life," I said as I pointed down with my index finger.

But she looked uncomfortable with the praise, even when it was coming from her older self. "I don't know," she said under her breath. "There's nothing I can do at this point."

"I know you think that," I said, "But I want you to know that this chapter will end. This isn't how your story unfolds. You haven't even got to the good part of your book."

A glimmer of hope briefly crossed her face. "I hope so because right now that seems like a lifetime away," she said.

We chatted for a few more minutes and then I told her I had to go. It was nice talking with Miss 23. I could easily be her best friend. Her genuineness was refreshing. Maybe that's what we all need to aim for, the ability to be our own best friends?

As we said our goodbyes I gave her a tight hug. "There is so much goodness coming your way. Just stay strong and know that no matter how anyone treats you, you are more than that."

She looked uncomfortable and didn't know what to say, so she simply said, "Thanks," and walked towards the door.

As I walked back to my office I realized that going back to that period had made me feel heavy and sad. I wrapped my arms tightly around myself. "We've come a long way," I whisper.

Chapter 14
Then

South Boulder Court

I settled into mediocrity like a caged animal settles into the zoo. I tried to leave Ricky several times over the next decade, but each time, he begged me to change my mind and I eventually caved. I tried to convince myself that the hassle of getting a divorce would be too much. If I was being totally honest with myself, I was worried that no one else would find me lovable. The idea of being alone was scarier than being alone together.

I had surrendered my personal happiness, but I refused to let my long-term career goals die along with it. I searched the country for inexpensive graduate programs and homed in on Arizona. I was determined to see my vision of being a therapist become a reality.

In order to afford graduate school, I had to pay in-state tuition. That meant living in Arizona for two years to establish residency before I even applied to school. I served my time as yet another gofer, this time at a mining company. I kept my eye on the ball, reminding myself that this was just a means to an end.

Luckily, all my patience paid off when I was finally able to go to graduate school. I felt ecstatic to finally be doing something *I* wanted for once in my life. Those were the best years of my life. Ricky was making a minimal salary, so I took out the maximum amount of student loans possible to fill the gap. I left graduate school with new vigor (and lots of debt). The world was my oyster. We bought our first home on South Boulder Court and I dived into the mental health world.

Out of the gate, I had some tough jobs. I worked in adoption and saw the pain and awe of both birth and adoptive parents. I worked in foster care and felt the struggle of children lost in the system. I worked in a state residential treatment center and saw foster kids who were so mentally ill and aggressive, they couldn't live in a foster home. My eye started to twitch while I worked there. A boy once barricaded himself in my office. Another child had to be restrained as he tried to run into oncoming traffic.

It wasn't surprising that I had a miscarriage while working there. The stress was taking its toll. Ricky and I had been trying to have a child for years and I had undergone many invasive procedures to finally get pregnant. After I got pregnant again I decided it was time to leave that job. I found my place as an infant and toddler mental health clinician, helping babies and toddlers navigate their new world. Working with babies who were abused, neglected or addicted to drugs was difficult at times. Doing in-home therapy with court-ordered families also had its dicey moments, but it was still better than pickaxes and near deaths.

Towards the end of my pregnancy, I developed a blood clot

that put me into pre-term labor. Eventually they decided to induce me at 32 weeks. Although Chloe's Apgar scores were perfect and she showed no complications, she was a difficult baby from the get-go. She couldn't eat. Breastfeeding was a nightmare and even bottle feeding wasn't working. It seemed as if she was living in perpetual pain, and I couldn't fix it. She screamed non-stop for most of her waking hours, and she was less likely to projectile vomit if I fed her facing away from me. Things slowly improved, but it was an uphill battle. I began to realize that my toddler had more issues than many of the infants and toddlers I was treating at work.

It wasn't until my agency put me through post-graduate infant and toddler mental health training that I finally realized things were anything but typical at home.

One day in class we were going over behavioral dysregulation of toddlers. I was growing annoyed as I listened to the professor rattle off the signs and symptoms of dysregulation in infants and toddlers. I felt the program was pathologizing what I viewed as typical behavior. I didn't often speak up, but I couldn't hold it in any longer. My hand shot up and instantly my heart started to pound. I silently begged the professor to call on me before I chickened out.

I asked, "Isn't it normal for kids to do that though? I mean, my daughter is two and she does that all the time."

A look of concern seemed to dance across the professor's face, the wrinkles of expertise and knowing etched on her forehead. I could tell she was choosing her words carefully. "No, it's not normally common," she said gently, "unless there are other things going on."

I felt a warmth on my cheeks and nodded, not daring to ask any more questions. I couldn't focus for the remainder of class. *Other things going on? What does she mean?*

A few weeks later we took a class on an assessment tool that evaluated infant and toddler non-verbal distress signals. They were itemized and we had flash cards to learn how to recognize them. It was fascinating what you could learn from a baby's non-verbal gestures.

After the training, I went back to my desk and lazily stared at a framed picture of Chloe. She was about eight months old in the picture. My body froze as I did a double-take. She had over three clear distress signals in the picture. How did I miss that? I shoved the photo in my purse, hoping none of my colleagues had noticed. I was embarrassed. I was supposed to be a specialist and I hadn't realized my own child had a problem.

A few weeks later I couldn't find childcare and had to take Chloe to a meeting. She climbed all over the table and chairs and wouldn't sit still. She would dart for the door every time I took my eye off her. I felt as if all the infant and toddler mental health specialists in the room were analyzing my every move. I picked her up and she squealed a high-pitched scream that reverberated throughout the building. I felt my underarms go sticky. I was in a room with other toddler specialists, and I could not control my own toddler.

Later that day, a co-worker politely suggested that I schedule an early intervention assessment to make sure she was "doing okay." I was offended, but I made the call to my own agency for services. I worked for such a large agency that I didn't recognize the woman that came out to assess Chloe. I didn't tell her that I worked at the same agency. It just felt too awkward.

My social anxiety kicked up in high gear. Paro showed up on the scene. He wouldn't miss this for the world. He brought his megaphone. *They are going to realize you are inept. They're going to know that with all the skills you are supposed to have, you can't even handle your own daughter.* I sat quietly and awkwardly through the assessment as Paro screamed in my ear.

It was even more embarrassing when the following week I was paired up with the same consultant to go out to assess a new family. She smiled at me as we sat on the living room floor but then a wrinkle formed in between her eyebrows. "Hey, didn't I come to your house last week?"

Shit. I hadn't recognized her at first. I was so overwhelmed with anxiety that day I had hardly looked up. I fiddled with the carpet and mumbled, "Um yeah, I guess you did."

Inside I was mortified. What must she think of me? Paro pounced to answer my question. *And now you are going to assess someone else's kid. She is going to know you are a fraud.*

I was quieter than usual in the assessment. Lost between the role of being the expert this week and the parent from last week, I struggled to wear two hats at once, and wound up not wearing any at all.

Eventually I got a packet in the mail with the assessment results. It was weird to see one of our reports talking about *my* child. Chloe was diagnosed with sensory processing disorder, what they called sensory integration disorder back then. They recommended occupational therapy and feeding therapy. She was also diagnosed with "failure to thrive," as her oral sensitivities had caused her to lose weight and drop off the growth curve.

After that I grew increasingly self-conscious about my ability to parent and avoided going out. I lived in the community where I worked. When I would go out Paro would whisper, *What if you bump into one of the families you help? How do you think they'll feel when they see you can't even manage your OWN kid? How will they feel when they see your problems are even worse than their child's issues?*

I had no answers to those questions, so I chose to avoid everything I possibly could. As much as I wanted to go to the neighborhood pumpkin festivals or the firework celebrations, I hid at home instead. It felt too probable that I would run into a family I treated.

One day I went to Target to pick up a few things. I was running out of time and needed to take Chloe with me. My heart was already pounding before we even got to the store. Her sensory issues made car seats and shopping carts intolerable. She wanted to be free, but if I let her walk, she would take off running. If I held her in my arms, she would arch her back, crying to get down. It would be a fight, no matter what I tried.

As we got into the store I grabbed a shopping cart. "Weee!" I said as I swirled her around and picked her up, trying my best to make it fun. "In you go," I said, trying to put her fighting feet into the cart. Her body went stiff, and she started to arch. A small trickle of sweat started to form under my shirt. "Sit, honey," I said, my eyes darting around to see who was watching us. *How do other parents do this?*

On cue she started to scream, "No! No!" her shrill so loud I was sure the entire store could hear her.

"Shhhh!" I snapped, glancing around. I held her on my hip with one hand as she forcefully tried to flip herself upside down. I used my other hand to grab the cart and moved towards an empty aisle. "We are doing this today," I told her between gritted teeth. I had bailed so many times before and I was determined to stick with it this time.

I tried to put her back in the cart. Her high-pitched scream continued to echo throughout the store. I felt my shirt starting to cling to me and my face was burning with embarrassment. Paro made an announcement in my ear. *You are making a scene. If anyone you know sees this, they will lose all respect for you.*

I ignored the berating and continued. "You have to sit!" I forcefully whispered. I was getting more panicky. The fluorescent lights started to spin and I was feeling disoriented. I took her little legs and guided them one by one through the shopping cart as I held her stomach, pushing her arching back down. I blindly searched for the seatbelt to lock her in place as my other hand tried to keep her from moving. I found one side of the seatbelt and switched hands to desperately search for the other. She arched as far back as she could while giving her best hyena impression. Her face was beet red, and I'm sure mine was too. I grabbed the other strap and on the second try, finally heard a snap.

I stepped away from the shopping cart and took a deep breath. I felt as if I had just won a wrestling match with an alligator. Sweat dripped down my spine. I tugged at the front of my shirt a few times to get some cool air on my body. She wriggled and screamed, her body finally contained in the straps. Out of breath I explained, "I'm sorry, but if we go shopping, you have to sit."

I pulled myself together, wiped the sweat from my forehead, and continued down the aisle with a screaming toddler. I wasn't going to give up, even if it was mortifying. Eventually her screams gave way to loud vocal "Nos" and then eventually to blissful silence. As we got to the parking lot we did the same song and dance to get her back into the car seat. It was exhausting and humiliating. As I hurriedly tried to get her strapped in, her screams carried throughout the parking lot. I had visions of Child Protective Services being called. "Um yes, there is a crazy woman trying to kill her child in row 13 of the Target parking lot."

Guilty as charged, officer.

* * *

Entering motherhood woke up the beast that was Paro. He had been like elevator music playing in the background, but now he was like screamo blaring in my ears.

When you become a mom with social anxiety not only do you have to worry about what others think of you, but you have to worry about what they think of your child *and* of your parenting. It's a lot to handle.

Chloe was a major test for my anxiety. Even though I didn't realize I had social anxiety at the time, I knew that my stress level had shot through the roof when I became a mom.

I was in the living room chasing my daughter. Only one of us was having fun.

"Come here, let me brush your hair before we go," I said, grabbing the brush with one hand and trying to hold an underwear-escaping contortionist, with the other. She wriggled away easily and ran into the other room.

I sighed and blew my hair out of my face. "Well, at least put your clothes on. We have to go in a few minutes," I said, putting my hands up in the air. She came out holding her bear bear, her over-loved pink beanie bear, its nose bitten off. Her hair was knotted and sticking up in all directions. She was wearing a soft cotton sleeveless dress with her equally over-loved pink crocs.

I took one look and moaned, "No, honey, you can't wear that. It's cold out today. You need to put on a long-sleeve shirt and some pants."

She balled her little hands into fists and I could almost physically see her digging her heels into the floor, "No, I like this. I don't want to wear pants!"

My eyes darted to the clock and a shot of adrenaline spread through me. I had to be at work and I hadn't included this argument in my schedule. By now I knew I wasn't dealing with typical stubbornness or opposition. My daughter had SPD (sensory processing disorder) and no amount of discipline, bribing or punishment was going to change this behavior. In my desperation, I had tried it all.

The struggle wasn't her, it was me. I didn't want to send her to school looking like that. What would people think of me? She would be a walking poster child for all my failures. *Look at me, my mom can't brush my hair or get me to match. And for extra bonus points, I am wearing totally inappropriate clothes for the weather.*

The idea of people making assumptions based on her appearance made me want to hide. I wanted to stick a note on her forehead that read, "Sorry, I tried. But she has SPD," but I'm sure that would probably be frowned on as well.

Going out to dinner was altogether another nightmare. Prior to having a child, I was already self-conscious about going out to eat. I felt as if I was walking on stage, and everyone was staring at me. I would glance at the other tables and swear people were judging me. Paro would pipe in with some suggestions. *Maybe it's your hair? Maybe this restaurant is too hip and you don't fit in?*

And then there would be the ordering. I didn't want to make any special requests. No extra dressing on the side. No requests to hold the onions. If my order was wrong, I would eat it anyway. If I needed a refill, I would wait until it was offered. I didn't want to inconvenience the wait staff. I didn't want to be a bother.

And then came my first child. A child who could not tolerate being restrained. A child who could not sit in an overstimulated restaurant without becoming dysregulated. A child who would rather throw food across the restaurant than quietly place it in her mouth.

We had tried to eat out. I wanted to be like everyone else. But after several attempts where she screamed at the top of her lungs and threw food further than I thought a toddler was capable, we gave up. Or I should say, I gave up.

Ricky seemed clueless. He didn't notice the glares we got. He didn't concern himself with the young couple who were probably on their first date, or the exhausted couple who probably paid a babysitter so they could finally have some alone time.

But I was not given the gift of ignorance, I never am. I saw it all. I felt it all. And it was all just too much.

My answer to the new stresses of motherhood was to hide. We wouldn't go out unless it was a place where I knew my sensory-seeking toddler could run wild and free. We went to the zoo and the children's museums and avoided restaurants and movie theaters.

But one place I couldn't avoid was pre-school. I signed her up for Montessori, hoping she would have more freedom with self-directed learning. I found a small school that only had 45 students. I thought the intimacy would be perfect for her. I hadn't considered the impact that intimacy would have on my anxiety. I liked to hide in a crowd. I didn't want to know Billy's mom or Jessica's dad.

After-school pick-up was a nightmare for me. It was 2:55 p.m. Everyone was gathering around the small entrance to the one pre-school class at the end of the building. I started to walk up the sidewalk and saw the group huddling around. *Oh great, I'm early.*

Groups unnerved me and caused me to go into instant panic mode. I slowed my pace and glanced at my watch. Five more minutes. Five more excruciating minutes. I walked even slower. Could I kill five minutes walking a few more feet? It was worth a try. I slowed down even more.

Forty-five seconds later I was in the middle of the group. Moms were talking to each other, paired off in twos and threes. I felt conspicuous, naked and exposed. I suddenly didn't know what to do with my hands or my body. This is what happens when I'm in groups. I shift my weight and yawn, trying to look more casual. It didn't work.

Paro must have got an emergency alert on his phone because he swiftly moved in. *Why do they all already know each other? It's as if they've all bonded at some secret club meeting you weren't invited to. You are late to the party. You'll never make friends with these moms.*

I tried to drown out his taunts and reached for my phone. I lazily scrolled through my emails trying to look busy. I glanced at the time. Three more minutes. Time was molasses and I felt stuck. I glanced up, trying to look natural. I quickly surveyed the group. Was anyone staring at me? Was anyone thinking I looked awkward? Paro answered, *Yes and yes! You couldn't be more awkward right now. How long are you going to stare at your phone? Why does this always happen to you? No matter where you go you don't fit in. It's as if you repel people.*

He was right. This does always happen to me. I always felt like the odd one out. I tried to fill in the missing piece of the puzzle in my mind. Maybe they all knew each other from some mommy's group I didn't join or maybe they all lived in the same neighborhood? My daughter had been enrolled in the school for three days and I was already feeling isolated and alone.

I looked at my phone. It read 2:59. I breathed a sigh of relief. This nightmare would soon be over, at least until tomorrow. I saw the door to her class crack open and then ten seconds later the kids came streaming out. I instantly felt relief, as if someone had been holding my throat and finally decided to let me breathe. I gulped in the air and scanned the little people for Chloe. I found her in the sea of children and gave her a hug. I felt relieved I had something to focus on other than my phone.

"Hey, honey! How was your day?" I asked, taking her backpack and moving towards the car.

"Waaait!" she cried. "I want to wait for my friend."

The hand on my throat started to tighten again. "No, honey. We really have to go," I nudged, trying to walk towards the direction of the car.

She let go of my hand and took off in the opposite direction. I stood there feeling awkward again. Parents were still gathered around talking, probably sharing numbers and arranging playdates. I stood alone.

I moved through the crowd, my blood boiling underneath my calm facade. I couldn't believe she was doing this. I was livid. I just wanted to go home.

I found her in the classroom. I tugged on her arm. "Chloe, come on. We need to go."

"Wait!" she said, as she tried to get another child's attention.

That's when I lost it. All my anxiety morphed into rage. I impatiently grabbed her hand and moved her back outside. I knelt down and angrily whispered in her ear, "We are leaving now!" I was sure every parent at the school was watching me unravel.

I navigated her through the maze of parents and kids, inching my way to the parking lot.

Suddenly Chloe tugged her hand away and started running in the opposite direction. "Here she is, Mom!" she said, pointing to a girl a few feet behind us.

"Hi, Sarah!" Chloe squealed. Sarah, an impeccably dressed five-year-old, just stared at her, no shared adoration on her face. "Mom, this is Sarah!" she said, trying to introduce us.

"Oh, hi, Sarah," I said. The little girl's blonde hair blew in the wind, her blue eyes wide open, confusion on her little face.

"Come on, Chloe, it's time to go," I said, trying to grab her hand again, this time talking more gently.

Chloe ignored my hand and skipped off ahead, happy she had found her "friend." My heart sank. I could tell that the little girl didn't like my daughter. I could tell she didn't want to even acknowledge her.

I wanted to cocoon her and protect her from the feelings of rejection and hurt that I had felt as a child. I wanted to whisper in her ear, *Don't pick that one, she doesn't like you.* But sometimes we can't share what we know or what we feel.

Was my social anxiety skewing my perceptions or did I have an innate ability to read the subtle social cues that she was missing? My cloudy perspective wouldn't let me know for sure.

I felt as if history was repeating itself, only this time I had to relive the feelings of rejection and isolation through the eyes of my daughter. It was torture to the power of two.

Chapter 15
Now

After the butterfly field trip, I started to feel more empowered to work on my social anxiety. Over the next year, I pushed myself as if I was preparing for a social anxiety marathon. I was frustrated that I had given my power away once again. I took a magnifying glass to my life and looked under every rock and crevice searching for Paro.

Where was he hiding? Where was he convincing me to feed him? I had done so much work four years prior after I published my first book. I had thrown myself into the public eye and exposed myself over and over again to diarrhea-worthy moments of anxiety. And yet, with the snap of Paro's fingers, I was back on my knees.

My new game was called "push Natasha out of her comfort zone." I had played it before, long ago when I had made all my initial progress. But it was time to play again.

I stared at the message and read it again. "Hey, Natasha! Are you going to the International OCD Foundation [IOCDF] conference this year?" A sinking feeling started to creep in, like when the creepy music in a horror movie starts to play and you know something bad is about to happen.

And then I heard it. *You have to go, Natasha. You can't avoid it this year. Not now, not with everything you've promised yourself.* I had a new voice in my head; a voice that liked to compete with Paro and torture me just as much. She was peppy and bold and told it to me straight. She bossed me around and convinced me it was for my own good. I knew she was right, but I still didn't like her. I argued with her often. *I'm too busy right now. And besides, do we really want to spend some of our summer vacation at an OCD conference?* But she was relentless. *If it makes you uncomfortable, then you'll have to go. You know the rules. Anything you're avoiding because of Paro you HAVE to do. There's no disputing that and you know it.*

I knew she was right. That's why the message made me so nervous. I had no choice. This was like the butterfly museum field trip on steroids. I typed back as quickly as I could. "Yup, I'll definitely be there! I hope to meet you in person finally," I replied, hitting the send button before I had time to change my mind.

The minute I sent it I wanted to take it back, but it was too late. I stared at the screen as I saw three little dots taunting me. She was typing back. No backing out now.

"Looking forward to seeing you there!" she typed.

I wanted to feel the same, but Paro instantly flashed a nightmarish scene in my head. He was the sole producer of my nightmares and he had talent. He had full access to all my insecurities and flipped through them as if they were flash cards for his script. One of his masterpieces played in my mind:

"Are you Natasha?" a woman asked.

"Yes, I am," I answered nervously, not knowing what to say.

"We love your stuff! I love your YouTube channel and podcast," she said. "Remember I emailed you about my daughter?"

I racked my brain to remember an email about a woman's daughter, but I was coming up blank. Just at that moment, another person called from across the room.

"Natasha? Hey, it's me, from your Facebook group." She gave me a tight hug and I awkwardly hugged her back.

"Oh hi!" I said, not recognizing her face. I mentally tried to scan through the 18,000 members in my group as she talked. I got nothing.

"...and I really appreciated that advice you gave me last week. It really helped," she said, starting to notice my lack of participation in the conversation.

I stood there speechless, not knowing what to say or how to carry on the conversation. I could see disappointment flash across her face. She wasn't impressed. I've never been impressive in real life, and now she knows the truth.

"Well anyway, it's been nice seeing you," she said.

I fumbled for my words. "You too," I attempted to say, but she was already walking away.

My heart was racing as the room started to come into focus again. Paro is good at what he does. He knows where to attack. He knows my vulnerabilities.

He's right, my biggest fear is being recognized. I had devoted my last four years to creating global resources for parents raising kids with anxiety or OCD and I did this in a very public way. I had a growing YouTube channel, and my podcast was often listed as one of the top 50 parenting podcasts on iTunes. I taught online anxiety and OCD classes where my face was splattered across every lesson. If I wanted to hide, especially in the OCD community, I was doing a piss poor job of it. There was no way I would be able to be a fly on the wall at that conference, even if I tried.

Also, I would be expected to go. It would seem weird if I didn't. Here I was, this OCD child expert who parents followed and looked up to and yet I couldn't even face my own fears and attend the conference. The irony would not be lost.

Normally I do the knee-jerk reaction that most people do when struggling with anxiety and I fight back. I argue with my anxiety, I tell myself it won't be that bad, that I can handle it. But these were platitudes and an ineffective way to handle vicious enemies like Paro. No, I had to be more strategic than that. I had to unravel his entire plan of attack. So, after his reel of terror was over, I made my first move.

So what if people recognize me? What's the worst that can happen? That I stumble on my words? That I don't know who they are? So what? Yes, it will be an awkward few minutes, but then I'll move on. Learning how to handle discomfort gets rid of YOU.

Paro didn't like this pivot. He didn't like me reacting to his prediction with calm and acceptance. He went in for the kill. *Can you imagine what it will feel like when you are just sitting there all alone in those sessions? No one to talk to, no one to be friendly with? People will think you are such a loser. They'll say, "Isn't that Natasha Daniels sitting there all by herself? I thought she was a somebody, but I guess she's really a nobody."*

I recoiled at the thought. Paro, sensing victory, pounced in and rolled his next reel of images in my mind. *Pretty uncomfortable Natasha, right?!* He taunted. *You can still back out. You have time.*

I took a breath and made my move. *So what if I'm alone. I am working on not caring what people think. Even if they think those things, what I think is the only thing that matters. I no longer define myself by how others see me. I get to define me. I can sit alone and handle the discomfort.*

I listened for a while, but Paro was silent. He didn't like this conversation and had retreated. He knew when he was losing a battle and he went to lick his wounds in private.

* * *

The flight was booked and the hotel was reserved, there was no going back now. Jimmie had offered to make it a family trip. He was always one to want to protect me.

"It will be fun," he offered. "I'll hang out with the Daniels fam and you can take the kids to the conference. We can meet up for dinners each night."

The idea brought instant calm to my nerves. Jimmie had tons of family in Texas, and I told myself that it did make logistical sense to combine the trip. But I knew deep down I was lying to myself. Jimmie coming with me was like putting on a wetsuit while I was trying to get used to swimming in the cold. It was a crutch, and his presence would envelop me with protective warmth.

To add to my growing number of social anxiety challenges, I had received several requests from people wanting to do presentations together. I happily agreed, feeling honored and petrified at the same time.

I had avoided these conferences for years, using the excuse that I had young children or that it was too far. I soaked up these lies because to think anything other than that would be to face my demons, and I hadn't been ready for that.

So when others asked me to present with them, I had no idea what to expect. I told myself that these were just submissions, and the odds of getting picked were very small. Two were approved. Two too many for my anxiety. I reminded myself that I was all in and that when I take on a challenge, I take it on big.

Jimmie was good at making all the logistical plans. We complemented each other that way when we traveled. I loved researching all the culture and fun activities we could do, and he loved to plot and plan our every move.

"So the conference will be here," he pointed on Google Maps, as he zoomed in with his fingers. "And we'll be right over here, just a block away. That way you can come and relax back at the hotel whenever you need a break." He had planned for us to stay at a hotel away from the conference so I could hide when I needed to.

"That sounds good," I said, feeling grateful that he did all the work for me. He knew me and he knew that this conference was going to overwhelm me, probably more than even I was willing to admit.

As we walked into the lobby of our hotel I instantly felt conspicuous. What if people are staying here as well? I glanced around to see if anyone was staring at me. I suddenly had an urge to hurry up and get our room keys.

Every bone in my body wanted to hide in the hotel room and not come out until the next day. I turned to Jimmie. "Let's put our bags away and then go check in at the conference," I said, ignoring Paro's overt nudge to start feeding him.

We walked the block to the hotel where the conference was being held. Swarms of people were buzzing about, like worker bees around a busy hive. I whispered to myself that it didn't matter how others defined me, it only mattered how I defined myself.

And how do you define yourself? My high-spirited, pushy Natasha Version 2.0 whispered to me. It was nice to hear her voice for once. I was going to need her in my ear this trip.

I am strong and I am kind. I may not be very social, but that's okay. I am an introvert and that has nothing to do with social anxiety. I don't enjoy small talk or getting to know large groups of people. I like deep, genuine, one-on-one connections. That doesn't make me a loser when I am sitting alone. That doesn't make me a social reject when I am not talking to others. It makes me who I am, and that's okay.

Good! I heard Natasha Version 2.0 say. *So act like it. Go in there with your head held high.* I was starting to really like her.

I was surprised at the ease I felt navigating through the crowds. We got my badge and my conference material and headed back to the hotel.

The next morning we got ready to walk over to the conference. My stomach was in knots. Paro was revolting, trying to wear me down. *It's too late!* I quietly screamed. *The trigger has been pulled.*

I weaved in and out of the crowd. It had been a big turnout

that year, almost two thousand people. I started to feel disoriented and overwhelmed by the organized chaos around me. I never did well in crowds. I noticed some familiar faces as I walked around. Natasha Version 1.0, the Paro edition, would have avoided all eye contact. She would have pretended to look at the schedule or glance at her phone to read an imaginary text.

My challenge wasn't to make this conference a white-knuckle ride, it was to fully immerse myself in it. My mind flashed back to what I tell my son when he's facing his fears about going upstairs alone, "Don't run into your room and then run downstairs as if your life depended on it. Go slow. Show your anxiety that there is nothing to be afraid of. Otherwise, all you're teaching your brain is that you dodged the imaginary knife-wielding attacker. That's not reprogramming your anxiety. That's not teaching your brain anything new."

I needed to heed my own advice. I was here to show Paro that I could handle discomfort. That I could sit naked in a crowded room and be okay. I lifted my head up and stared at others as they walked past me. I smiled at a few, some smiled, but some didn't smile back. A simple perceived rejection like that would have spiraled my social anxiety into a deep dark pit of concern and embarrassment. But this time, I shrugged it off and moved on.

I dropped my kids off at the children's session and carried on alone. I felt more vulnerable and naked without them. With the cloak of my children's company, I felt less exposed to the harsh elements around me.

I re-centered myself. *I can do this. These aren't sharks and I'm not drowning in the deep sea. These are people. They aren't focused on me and what I'm doing. They have their own thoughts, their own places to be.*

I made my way to the first session. It was crowded. I didn't hide in the back row as Paro demanded. I walked down the center aisle and found a seat. My kneejerk reaction was to pull out my security blanket and pretend to look at my phone. But I kept it firmly in my pocket. *No white knuckling*, I reminded myself.

I was surprised at how easily I was able to immerse myself in the topic being discussed. My mind wondered not about who was staring at me, but about the therapeutic approaches they discussed and how I could apply them to my practice. I was deep in Paro territory, but he no longer had the mic. The silence made me giddy with hope.

The next few days were a whirlwind of activity and conversations. Early in the conference I had met up with my friend Patricia, a colleague I had met online through my OCD work. She was warm and friendly and put me right at ease. She was a cold glass of water when this challenge overheated me.

"Where are you?" she would text.

"In Room C. Where are you?" I'd reply.

"Coming towards you. Save me a seat," she wrote.

It felt like a warm blanket to have a genuine friend in the sea of strangers. It was fuel that kept me going when I was alone.

As the conference progressed, I gained more confidence. I no longer felt uncomfortable walking among the large crowds of people alone. Even when people would stop me to talk about my podcast, YouTube videos, or Facebook group, I welcomed the conversations, even if some of them felt a bit awkward. It was okay to feel awkward. It was okay to not recognize someone. It was okay to not know where to take the conversation. I was learning how to welcome my discomfort and each time I did, Paro lost a little bit of his bark.

The last day of the conference I had to present. The first presentation was a panel, and I was surprised that I was actually looking forward to it. When I got into the room my heart wasn't racing and I casually pushed the microphone closer to my mouth, waiting for the presentation to begin. I wondered who this Natasha Version 2.0 was. I barely recognized myself.

My final presentation was a workshop with kids. That's my comfort zone. Put me in a group of kids and all my social anxiety goes away. I could talk to a zillion kids and never get nervous. They are my people and with them I feel completely at home. I did the workshop with another colleague I had met online. Doing it with another therapist put me at ease. We took turns teaching the kids and the time passed quickly.

As we packed up and said our goodbyes, I realized that I wished the conference wasn't ending. I actually enjoyed teaching the kids and surprisingly liked meeting people from the OCD community in person. I felt connected and bonded to all these people. I could feel the compassion and love in the air, and it felt like the closest thing I had felt to belonging.

* * *

I sat back in my big armchair and sipped my coffee. "It's nice to get to talk to you," I said to Miss 34, who was sporting a pixie haircut and dark maroon lipstick. She was a younger, more youthful version of myself. She looked tired and worn out.

"So, tell me, how's life going?" I asked.

She sighed deeply, probably knowing that she wouldn't be able to bullshit the older version of herself. I could tell she was contemplating which way to take this session. She finally spoke, "It's frustrating. I feel that I made some bad choices and now I'm stuck."

I knew what she was talking about but nudged her to elaborate. "Like what?" I asked.

"Well, I was in such a rush to not be alone, I jumped at the first opportunity to escape my feelings of rejection and hurt." She stared off, deep in thought. "I also just wanted to grow up and start my own life. But this isn't what I had pictured," she said, motioning to an invisible life she felt trapped in.

"So why don't you change that? You are in charge of your own destiny," I challenged, knowing she would argue this.

"I know, but it's hard. I now have a toddler and I'm the only one holding us together financially. I don't even think I can afford to get a divorce," she said. "How sad is that?"

"You can," I said, but I didn't argue further. I knew in a few short months something devastating would happen to her that would change her whole perspective. But until then, it wasn't worth talking about.

"How is motherhood and working full time?" I asked.

"It's been hard. First of all, I'm exhausted. I work long hours and then I come home and have no energy to spend with Chloe. Also, I feel as if I am failing." She looked away when she said the last part.

"Failing? In what way?" I probed.

"My daughter's issues are out of control. I can't even feed her. She is dropping off the growth chart and no one can give me answers. Also, to be honest, I'm embarrassed to take her places. I can't manage her easily."

I leaned in closer and patted her knee. "Let me tell you something. Any parent would have a hard time managing her sensory processing needs. You don't realize that because she's your only child right now, but her issues are extreme." I could tell that my words were easing her guilt a bit.

"Second," I continued, "your social anxiety has just been seriously triggered by motherhood. So on top of all that, you are ultra-sensitive to feeling embarrassed or judged right now."

She nodded. "I am, but I don't think it's social anxiety. I just think that anyone would feel awkward if they couldn't control their own kid."

I thought, *Even now, after all this time, she still doesn't realize she has social anxiety.*

"You know you have social anxiety, right?" I blurted out.

She looked off kilter. "I...I don't think so," she said, contemplating my diagnosis.

I took off my kid gloves for the adult version of myself. "Okay, so then tell me why you always feel as if people don't like you? Why do you feel so conspicuous around other moms?" I challenged.

She shrugged. "Honestly, I just repel people. I think I always have. I am not sure why, but I am just not the kind of person people want to be close friends with. If people had a choice in a group of people, I would be the last pick."

I shook my head. "Nope. Those are lies you are telling yourself," I said flatly.

I could tell she was growing frustrated with me. "No, it's true. It has happened time and time again. You can go through my whole history and see this pattern play over and over again," she argued.

I leaned in and spoke slowly. "Trust me, I have, in minute detail." I thought about all the sessions I'd had with all my previous selves. "And you will eventually find out that you are wrong."

She put her hands up. "So then why do I repel people?"

I thought about it for a minute. "For a lot of reasons, really. First, you are so consumed with how others see you that you never get lost in the moment, you are always lost in your head. You are always analyzing your interactions as they happen. That can make you a bit awkward," I explained.

"Second, you are never friendly first. Ever," I added. "Think about it, have you ever in your life gone up to someone and been the first to start a conversation?"

She thought about it for a moment. "I guess...I haven't," she said.

I pointed my index finger at her. "You don't do that, and that limits you. It makes you unfriendly. It makes others get the message that you don't want to talk, that you don't want to be friends," I tried to explain.

She sighed, "Well, to be honest, I am kind of an introvert. I really don't like large groups of friends, and superficial friendships are the worst," she said.

"Yes, you are introverted, and you are very picky, but your social anxiety uses that against you," I said.

Her face wrinkled up like she was confused. "In what way?"

"You don't have to be introverted or picky to have social anxiety. That just happens to be your personality. But you hide behind that. You tell yourself that you aren't talking to others because you are introverted, when in reality some of the time it is because you are scared shitless of rejection."

She swallowed hard when I said that. I knew it had hit her to the core.

"I see," she said softly. "You're probably right," she conceded.

Feeling bad at how direct and blunt I had been, I tried to soften what I said next. "I am only telling you this because you can't get better until you take a step back and see the lies that social anxiety has been feeding you. You've been on automatic pilot for 34 years, not even knowing that social anxiety was at the helm. You need to see reality for what it is in order to be able to make the changes necessary to improve."

She nodded in agreement. I could tell she was opening up to my perspective.

I gave her a faint smile and continued, "You want to know what is ironic?"

She looked at me and shrugged.

"How often have you had these conversations with kids in your practice? You have always been so skilled at spotting social anxiety and yet you are blind to your own."

"It's true. I can see social anxiety a mile away," she agreed.

I leaned in and hit both my knees. "Exactly! You *can*. That's what makes you so good at what you do. You have a skill at getting others to see what is right in front of them. You know how to sprinkle that insight and empower kids to feel confident in their own skin." I looked down at my feet and shook my head. "I only wish you would do that for yourself," I looked up with tears in my eyes, "for us."

It was getting late, and I needed to end our session to start my real work day.

She grabbed her purse and stood up.

As she headed for the door I said, "Oh, one more thing. You know that festival psychic who told you that you would take a sharp turn at 34?"

"Oh yeah," she said with a smile. "I remember that. I don't see any sharp turns happening anytime soon," she laughed, shrugging. "I don't think she was that good. She also said I would have two more kids. I told her I was practically infertile and Chloe was a complete miracle."

"Yeah, I remember," I said, thinking to myself, *She might have been better than you thought.*

Chapter 16
Then

Piñon Court

My eyes were heavy and I was dragging myself to the phone. We had just made our first trip across the big pond to take Chloe to England. Taking her across the world was like five nightmarish visits to Target all balled up in one. Trying to contain her on the plane was like trying to hold a squirrel for eight hours.

We made it to Ricky's parents' house and put our bags down in one of their small bedrooms. All I wanted to do was fall on one of those tiny beds and sleep for days, but I couldn't. His mom walked in and said I had a phone call.

Instinctively I brought my hands to my heart. Why would anyone be calling me here?

I swallowed hard and put the cold receiver to my ear, "Hello?"

"Tash, it's Aunt Michele. Sorry to bother you, I know you've just arrived in England," she said in her strong Brooklyn accent. I knew something was wrong. My aunt would never call me here.

"That's okay, is everything alright?" I asked, waiting for the grenade to drop.

"Yeah, yeah, don't worry," she started. "Your mom wanted me to call you because she had to be admitted to the hospital."

I grabbed the back of my neck and my legs felt shaky. "Is she okay? What happened?"

"Please, don't worry about it. She had an asthma attack and they are just keeping her for observation," she said. "She'll be fine."

I was confused. Why would they be keeping her for observation? Something didn't make sense. "What are they observing?" I asked.

"They just want to make sure her heart is okay. But she's fine. She's sitting up and talking."

She was trying to calm my nerves. I twirled the phone cord nervously around my finger. "Do you think I should come back?"

She sighed heavily into the phone, "Well, I'll tell you what. Let's just see how she does and I'll call you back in a bit."

About an hour later she called back and said I should get home as soon as possible. Ricky's mom helped me make flight arrangements. Ricky wanted to stay with Chloe and carry on with the trip. Normally that would bug me, but this time I was glad. I didn't know what was waiting for me at home, but I knew I'd want to give my full attention to it.

The next week was a blur. My mom hadn't been having an asthma attack, she had been having a heart attack. When she came into the ER and said she was having a hard time breathing, they misdiagnosed her and gave her albuterol without screening for a heart attack. They pressed the fast forward button on her demise. A few heart surgeries later, she was sitting in a medically induced coma in the recovery room, too fragile to be moved to the intensive care unit.

For the first few days we all sat in a small waiting room lined with chairs, a muted TV nailed to the corner of the wall. We weren't a big family, so we all packed in quite easily. My aunt and uncle, Joel, Allison, Leigh, Jake, my dad and my grandma. My dad would tell a story or make a comment and then a few minutes later he would tell it again, with no memory that he had just said it. Life was on a nightmarish loop and I couldn't turn it off.

After a week of limbo, I was told to go home. They would call if anything changed. My mom, who was always afraid of death, was having a gruesome ending. At 59, she continued to lie in the recovery room, still too frail to be moved. After an allergic reaction to a blood thinner, clots formed throughout her body. They had to amputate her leg and were now discussing amputating her arm. They were taking her away bit by bit.

I called Ricky from the surgery waiting room before going home. "Things aren't looking good here," I said. "She is in a medically induced coma."

"Sorry, Tash," he said.

I stayed quiet on the phone, exhausted and unable to string my words together. "Yeah, it's been a long few days. I'm exhausted," I managed to say.

And then his tone shifted, as it often did. "Well, aren't you going to ask about your daughter and how *we* are doing?" His voice suddenly sounded accusatory and hostile.

I bit my cheek and gripped the phone tighter. I didn't even know how to respond to this. "I am assuming you are both doing well. I've been busy with what is going on here," I said.

"Well, you would think you'd want to know how your daughter is doing. After all, you just left us here," he said. "We went to Stratford-upon-Avon yesterday. We rode the carousel. She really loved it, Tash. We fed the ducks and..."

His voice faded into the distance as the sound of my boiling blood drowned him out. I was fuming. I cut him off, "I didn't just leave you, my mom is dying. You got to be fucking kidding me right now. I shouldn't have to worry about Chloe. She's with her dad. I should be able to shelve that right now and focus 100 percent on my mom." I looked around the waiting room, realizing I was shouting. I didn't care.

"I just can't even talk to you right now. Don't call me back, I don't want to talk to you," I said as I hung up the phone, wishing there was a way to slam down a cell phone.

Our marriage hadn't been on the rocks, it had been on the boulders. Before our trip to England I had given him an ultimatum: either change or I was leaving. I insisted that we go to therapy, and he said he wouldn't go. He didn't know it at the time, but that would be the nail in our marital coffin.

I flew back to Arizona and sat in an empty house waiting for the phone to ring. The silence was welcoming, but it wasn't long before my sister called. She was sobbing and I knew what she was going to say before she said it. "Sorry, Tash," she said between gasps, "Mom didn't make it." She choked on the last sentence.

Hearing the finality in those words startled the foundation

under my feet. Even though each one of us had a rocky relationship with my mom, she was the glue that kept our dysfunction together, and it was going to unravel fast. She was the only person I could fully depend on. She had come to my rescue countless times when I was a teenager and despite her selfishness, her number had always been on speed dial.

I felt bad that Leigh had to be the one to make the calls. She was left to hold down the fort as the rest of us went back to our places across the country. As it turns out, I would be making a similar call to her about my dad in the years ahead.

Ricky and Chloe arrived back home and the house became chaotic again. I escaped into my work, searching for solitude in the distraction.

I became consumed with the thought that my mom didn't live out her life's potential. She got married at 19 to a man she told me she hardly liked and lived a life feeling trapped and confined. Was I doing the same exact thing? Was I destined to live a mediocre life, with a man I didn't love? Was I going to remain a prisoner in a life that stifled my growth only to die a life of unlived potentials, like she had?

I had been so afraid to live a life of loneliness that I bit at the first opportunity that came my way. I didn't think anyone would find me worthy enough for love, but I forgot the power in loving myself.

Within weeks of burying my mom, I buried my dying marriage too. I was done. Done with settling for mediocrity. Done with thinking I wasn't good enough to deserve more. Done with worrying about everyone else's well-being at the expense of my own.

Ricky chalked it up to my grief, devaluing the depth of thought I had put into making the decision.

"You just aren't thinking right," he said. "I know you are having a hard time with your mom's death."

I wanted to punch him. I dug my nails into the couch so I would not lunge at him. He always misunderstood me, why did I think this would be any different?

We were broke, so getting a divorce lawyer was not an option for either one of us. There was nothing left to fight over except debt. I just wanted out.

"Keep everything," I said. "All I want is the Keurig coffee pot."

After working long hours, I came home and researched how to file for divorce without an attorney. Where there is a will, there is a way. I found a DIY website and went to the courthouse to file my handwritten paperwork. I paid for us to go to a mediator to create a parenting plan. I went to court alone to finalize our divorce.

I had spent my whole life avoiding where I finally found myself—completely alone. My emptiness was not hidden behind a loveless marriage. My loneliness was not concealed by a warm body sitting across from me at a restaurant. I was truly alone. I had no close friends, no close relatives, no neighbors to check on me.

"Mommy, are you ready?" Chloe asked. It was Christmas time and I had promised her we would go to see the zoo lights.

"Yup, just give me a sec," I said, wiping down the granite countertop. I kept my new home immaculate. After living in uncontrollable filth for 12 years, I was in neat freak heaven. My house always looked like a model home.

But there had been some major sacrifices to get the solitude I was now enjoying. I was in financial ruin from the divorce and the short sale that followed. I was under more pressure to pay a larger mortgage and had to work even longer hours. And the loneliness I had spent my whole life keeping at bay had finally arrived. I had never lived by myself. Not while I was in college or at any other time in my life. I always had the chitter chatter of someone else in the house. It was like background music that kept my darkest thoughts away.

I lifted Chloe into her car seat as she squealed with delight. "Can I get cotton candy?" she asked.

"We'll see," I said, buckling her up and kissing the top of her head. It was a busy night at the zoo. Signs for overflow parking began before we even got close. I felt my body stiffen. I hated crowds, they always made me feel so self-conscious and overwhelmed.

I realized that I had never been anywhere like this alone. People were like a life raft for my social anxiety. As long as I was with someone, I was immune from the tsunami of insecurity that would drown me. But I was out in the deep sea and there was no life raft in sight.

We pulled into the makeshift gravel parking lot several miles away from the zoo. I felt jittery and nervous.

"You'll need to hold my hand the entire time if you are not in your stroller, okay?" I told Chloe as I pulled the umbrella stroller out from the trunk.

"Okay!" she said, staring at the crowds lining up for the zoo shuttle.

I had the sudden urge to turn around, get in the car and go back to the warmth of my immaculate house. My panic was starting to send an emergency signal throughout my body. I took a deep breath and forced my legs to walk towards the buses. "Let's go have some fun!" I said, hoping to convince both of us.

Families were lined up to take the shuttle. We took our spot in line and I looked ahead of us. *God, this is going to take forever.* I popped open the stroller and told Chloe to hop in.

"Nooooo!" she screamed. "I'm walking. I promise I'll hold your hand." She squirmed out of my arms.

Even though Chloe had just turned four, she was still hard to manage, especially in crowds. "Please, just sit until the shuttle comes," I begged. "We might be here for a while." I reached to grab her again.

The promise of it being temporary appeased her and she allowed me to lift her into the stroller. I looked around, already exhausted. Did people see me struggling with her? As I glanced around the crowd a sinking feeling took over. Couples were holding hands. Dads carried their toddlers on top of their shoulders as moms held out cameras to get the perfect shot. Laughter echoed in my ears, almost mocking me.

The noise and chaos woke Paro up. *Have you noticed that*

there is no one here alone? Look around. You're the only one without friends or family, just standing here with your daughter all by yourself.

A lump in my throat made it hard to swallow. *You're right, I have no one. I am literally all alone in the world. I have no friendships. No best friends on speed dial. I have no close family here.* My thoughts went even darker. *If I were to die, how long would it be before anyone would notice? I am insignificant and the world wouldn't pause to miss my absence.*

The shuttle brought us to the front entrance. I lugged the stroller with one hand as I held Chloe with the other. We walked through the entrance around the large families standing in front of the sign that said "Zoo Lights," snapping what inevitably would be Christmas card photos.

As I walked past the crowds, a man ushered me to the wall. "Stand together," he said, a camera around his neck. Behind him was a backdrop of fake Christmas trees. I awkwardly put the stroller down and grabbed Chloe in my arms. She wriggled as I held her tight.

"One, two, three!" he said, as the big flash of his camera went off. "Here you go," he said, handing me a piece of paper with a number on it. "You can see your photo at the photo booth inside."

No thanks, I'd rather die, I thought.

The smell of caramel and maple syrup filled my nostrils as we passed the roasted nut stand. I spotted a trash can and threw the paper away. I didn't want a permanent memory of how I felt tonight.

I teared up as we walked around. I felt suffocated by the love and belonging that mocked me wherever I looked. A family wearing lit-up Christmas necklaces and matching red sweaters gathered in front of me to take a picture. I took Chloe's hand to walk around them. Another family in Christmas pajamas almost bumped into me. I felt invisible to the world.

Back home, I got under my warm blanket, wrapping myself up in the protected comfort of my cocooned world. I wiped the cotton candy sugar off of Chloe's face and got her ready for bed. She fell right asleep, the buzz of activity wearing her down.

I lay alone in bed, warm tears wetting my pillow. The room was as dark as my thoughts. *How did I end up here? At 35, how did I not have a soul to count on? How could I be so alone?* The freedom I got from leaving Ricky still felt liberating, but it hid a deeper truth. I had no one, and in truth that had been the case for a very long time.

* * *

Like Phoenix, I lived up to my city's name and rose up from the ashes, creating a new chapter for myself the following year.

In my quiet attempt to start anew, I sheepishly went onto eHarmony to find my long-lost soulmate. Having a solo private practice and a social life equal to that of a monk, I knew the odds of me meeting someone in person were worse than getting struck by lightning.

The universe threw me a gift when it matched me with Jimmie. He was everything I had been missing. He was considerate, funny and intelligent. When I saw his picture, it was as if I was staring at a long-lost friend. I felt as if I had seen that perfect smile and dark wavy hair with greenish hazel eyes before. He felt like home before I even met him.

We talked long into the night about things that mattered.

Paro didn't miss a beat. *He's too young for you. What does he see in you anyway? How embarrassing that you have a boyfriend. Are you back in high school?*

Ricky didn't help either. "You know this isn't going to last long, right? I just don't want to see you get hurt. He's just using you. What would a guy six years younger see in an older woman anyway?"

I grew annoyed. "You're just shallow, you wouldn't get it," I barked back. But secretly I worried about it too. Why did Jimmie like me? For once I was with someone who had so much to offer, but what did he want with me? Would I eventually disappoint him? Would he eventually realize that he was out of my league?

Jimmie worked as an FBI agent and lived in Vegas. Regardless of the fact that we both put filters on our profiles to stay within our states, we wound up getting matched. With my joint custody and his work assignment in Vegas, we were stuck with a long-distance relationship.

Jimmie and I both had our own insecurities. He worried I'd get back together with Ricky, and I worried he'd find someone else. He committed to flying back and forth every weekend. Within a year, we were engaged and married, but still living in two different states. I grew insecure that he wasn't doing enough to get a transfer to Phoenix.

Paro creeped his way into our relationship. He whispered

insecurities that would ooze into the cracks of our growing foundation. *He's not into you. His love is fading.* I got pregnant and Jimmie had still not asked for a transfer.

"I just want to ask when the time is right," he would say when we argued.

"Well, if having a pregnant wife isn't the right time, I don't know when is," I snapped back.

Eventually he did ask for the transfer, and when Xander was three months old we were finally under the same roof on Piñon Court.

Although Jimmie had a hard time being emotionally available, he was determined to make my life comfortable and easy. He knew me well and would make sure that I had all my creature comforts. He was dependable, loyal and always had my back. It felt refreshing to be with someone who completely got me. I finally felt whole for the first time in my life.

Paro found a new bone to maul on: Motherhood, Part 2. Jimmie and I had our first and second child in quick succession. I was a new mother at 40 and I felt just as uncomfortable in my motherhood skin as I did seven years prior. This time, however, I had the financial stability to provide for my kids, a luxury I was not given before. I also had a partner who fully supported me, and the privilege of hand-picking where I wanted them to go to school.

Twenty minutes from our house, through the mountainous desert, was a utopian Montessori school. It was perfect. There were vegetable gardens and shade trees with picnic tables. The kids learned Spanish and yoga. Classical music played in the background as kids sat on woven mats and did their tray work. I wanted them to stay there until college, not kindergarten.

But the moms intimidated me and put my social anxiety, once again, in overdrive. Much like every other social situation, I convinced myself that I was on the outside looking in.

We rode the big bumps on the desert road leading up to the school. "Go faster, Mommy!" Xander said from the back.

"More! More!" Alex chimed in. It made my stomach turn into knots, but I sped up for the last bump. "Weeeee!" both kids squealed with delight.

I drove into the crammed parking lot. It was always hard to find a space. I parked my Toyota between a Lexus and BMW. I looked at the sea of luxury cars surrounding me as I unbuckled Alex from her car seat and thought, *Maybe this is why I don't fit in? Look at these cars.*

Xander skipped ahead on the path as I walked Alex to her class. I always felt so conspicuous dropping the kids off. My eyes darted to the moms hanging around their cars or on the path, holding their coffee cups, catching up and arranging playdates. They made it look so easy.

"Hold on, wait for us," I yelled as Xander ran ahead. Coming from the other direction was a mom holding her phone and coffee. I wondered if I should smile or look away?

As she got closer I looked down at Alex and asked her an unnecessary question, "Are you going to have a great day?" She smiled back and nodded. I looked up, relieved the mother had passed. I dropped the kids off at their classes and started the walk back to the car. The walk back was even worse. I didn't have my tiny human shields to use as a distraction.

I focused on my walk. Am I walking weirdly? Do I look awkward? Paro piped in, *Here comes disaster the sequel. Another mom is going to pass you, let's see if you can make it even more awkward than the last one.*

I didn't like his tone. I didn't like being bossed around. I mustered up my courage and looked up at the mom, smiled, and said hi as I walked past her. She glanced over with a flat expression and kept walking.

It was a three-second interchange, or rather a one-way interchange, but it was enough material to fill up the 20-minute ride back home.

Well, that was dumb, Paro piped in. I had turned on the radio to distract myself, but he was just too loud. *They just don't like you, do they? Probably because you are old. That, or it could be because of how you dress? Or is it how you look? So many possibilities.*

Enough! I shouted back in my head. *All I did was say hi, can we just move on?*

But Paro never let me move on. He always sautéed me in rejection, making sure the pain was fully cooked.

Chapter 17
Now

I was finally catching up with myself, only a couple more sessions before time criss-crossed and I was with my present self. Even though Ms. 40 was only six years older than my last Natasha, life looked drastically different for her.

I walked out to the hall and smiled at her. "Hey, come on in!" It was like greeting my twin at the door. My body language mirrored hers, and we both gestured for the other to go in first.

She sat on the couch and found a place to put down her large Dunkin' Donuts coffee. I breathed in the aroma, remembering the joys of drinking gallons of coffee a day. Another thing anxiety and irritable bowel syndrome eventually took from me.

"So, how are things going?" I asked, perpetually struggling with how to begin.

But this was a more savvy, confident Natasha and she didn't need much of a runway to start a conversation.

"Much better. Who knew life could improve so drastically when we start to think about what we want for our life?" She leaned over and took a sip of her coffee, having a much more relaxed vibe than the last Natasha.

"I agree. You have spent most of your life thinking about everyone else. What does everyone else think? What does everyone else want? You spent so much time worrying about how everyone else was doing, you forgot about yourself."

She nodded her head in agreement. "You're right, I did. I never realized that until after my mom died. I sometimes wonder what would have happened if she hadn't died. Would I still be trapped in a marriage I never wanted?"

"You're seeing only one leaf on a newly sprouting tree. That marriage was only one small part of how you were holding yourself back. There was and is so much more. What do you think got you into that marriage to begin with? What got you to think that you were a second-class citizen who didn't deserve a place at the table?" I said, getting fired up. "Now, that's what you should really be asking," I challenged her.

"Well..." she started to say, trying to gather her thoughts. "I don't know if I hold myself back in other ways. Things are good now. I have a husband who I can actually talk to and who is a true friend. I don't feel alone anymore. And I have two more kids—who would have thought that was possible?" she joked.

"Well, apparently the festival psychic," I teased back.

"Oh God, you're right," she said, putting her hands to her face. "I remember arguing with her that it was literally impossible since I was having fertility problems," she laughed. "Thankfully I'm in a good place, and things are going well."

"How do you feel when you drop the kids off at Montessori?" I prodded.

"Well..." she nervously reached for her coffee again. "A bit out of place. I'm just not like those moms. I'm older, I'm not as affluent. You know, they really aren't my people."

I was annoyed that she couldn't go deeper, see the bigger picture.

"You've been selling yourself those lies since you were little," I said flatly. She looked wounded and I worried I had been too harsh.

"I don't know what you mean. I have to accept that not everyone is going to like me and I'm learning to be okay with that," she explained.

"Well, yes, that may be true. But you have spent 40 years denying the root cause of all this," I said, putting my hands out, exhausted with my alter ego.

"Denying what?" she asked, seeming to be equally exhausted with me.

I slapped my knees with my hands out of frustration and leaned in, "That you have social anxiety. You always find reasons why people don't like you. Why you repel people, right? That's what you always say, that you repel people. What if that were true but only for a completely different reason? What if your anxiety repelled people?"

"I don't know," she said, holding her coffee with two hands, trying to get warmth back into the room. "I don't want to use anxiety as an excuse."

I looked up at the ceiling in frustration. "Would you say that to one of the kids you are seeing in therapy?"

She stammered, "No, no, of course not."

"Then why can you say that to yourself?" I took a breath

and continued, "It's not an excuse, it's a reality. You sabotage friendships and interactions before they even begin. You are analyzing how it will go before they even start, before they even have a chance to start," I said.

She hid behind her coffee taking another sip and paused. "That's true. I do that."

"What do you think that looks like to the outer world? I can tell you what it doesn't look like. It doesn't look like a warm, inviting person wanting to connect and be friendly," I said, leaning closer to her.

She scooted back in her seat nodding her head back and forth. "Honestly though, I don't like to socialize. I am not a chatty, small talker. I find it quite draining," she explained.

"Yes, and that is 100 percent true, I'll give you that. But that is about you being an introvert, not about you having social anxiety," I said.

"But what's the difference? Maybe I'm just introverted, not socially anxious," she challenged.

I sighed and ran my hands through my hair. "People get those confused all the time. They think they're synonymous and they're not. You can be an introvert and not have anxiety at all. Just like you can have social anxiety and at your core be an extrovert," I tried to explain. "You happen to be both, but don't confuse one for the other," I cautioned. "Then you'll never get over your social anxiety and find your true self."

She put down her coffee cup and grabbed a couch pillow to hug. "My head is spinning. I have no idea how to separate the two. They feel the same to me."

"An introvert may not like small talk, but they don't get sweaty palms and heart arrhythmia when they are in a group of strangers. They can sit there quietly and not socialize and be okay with that," I explained.

She laughed out loud. "God, wouldn't that be nice? I couldn't even imagine. Just the idea of it makes me nervous."

"Yes, because you have social anxiety!" I pushed. "The goal isn't for you to socialize more, you don't even want that. The goal is for you to accept who you are and be comfortable in your own quiet skin, even when you are surrounded by a group of strangers," I said.

"But it's so hard when everyone else is talking and being friendly. I feel like such an outcast, such a loser," she said.

"Those are just beliefs. Beliefs your social anxiety doesn't want you to let go. What if you changed those beliefs? What if you embraced your true essence? When we change our beliefs, we also change our perceptions," I said. I leaned in closer and said in almost a whisper, "So what is another belief you can have when you are sitting alone in a group of strangers?"

She was silent for a bit. "Well, I prefer to skip the small talk. I am an introvert and I like to have deep, meaningful conversations with people. That means I'm slower to warm up and I'm slower to engage with someone new. But when I do, I often have a deeper, authentic connection and the conversation is more rewarding for both of us."

I slapped my legs with excitement. She was finally getting it. "Yes! Exactly! And you're not going to have too many of those and that's okay," I reminded her.

She didn't seem as enthused about the conversation as I was. "I just feel like the odd one out. I don't see other people just sitting there like that. It makes me feel awkward."

"Your social anxiety is going to point out all the friendly people, bonding and connecting. It's a powerful weapon to use and it's been effective. Who cares if other people are bonding and connecting. You do you," I said, pointing at her.

"You're right," she said shaking her head. "I guess I have to work on that."

I nodded in agreement, knowing that unbeknown to her, she was creeping up to the top of a rollercoaster ride and her battle with Paro was about to pick up some major speed.

Chapter 18
Then

Cavedale Drive

How often do we think we are at the end of the book and then find that there are more chapters to come? So much of life is filled with more twists and turns than we imagined. Whenever I think I am at the *happily ever after*, another sharp turn emerges in the road, one I usually have not seen coming.

So, 2015 was another sharp turn, just like 2006 had been when my mom died and I decided to jump off a cliff rather than remain in a dead marriage.

I thought I had reached my peak and that all I had to do was sail into the sunset. I had my private practice, a nice home we had built on Cavedale Drive, a partner I loved and three anxious, but happy, kids. I had been in private practice for ten years at this point, but whenever there was a small lull, I started to panic. What if my practice never thrived again?

While Jimmie and I showered together, I started to vent. "It's just weird. I only have four sessions today and three tomorrow. I'm just not filling up like I used to."

He put body wash on the loofah and started to wash my

back. "You say this every summer. Things slow down. People take vacations and travel in the summer. It will start to fill up once school starts. It always does."

He cupped his hands, pooled warm water in them, and poured it on my shoulders.

I turned around as he was cupping more water in his hands. "I say this every year?"

"Yes, every year, and it is always fine." He turned me around and hugged me. "Everything is fine," he whispered in my ear. "You are always waiting for the other shoe to drop, but what if it never does?"

He was right, I was always waiting for my picturesque world to crumble. Life felt too good and I was flinching, preparing for an invisible hit.

Even though his reassurance settled me, I still felt the need to take some action. One day, feeling bored in my office, I toyed with the idea of writing a book. I was never one to sit and soak up the slow pace life threw at me. I remembered receiving a catalog of therapy books and retrieved it from my shelf. I turned it over and there was an address to send submission requests. Perfect!

I did a quick survey of the market and realized there was a huge gap in toddler anxiety. There were no books solely on the topic. I had gone through all that infant and toddler mental health training when Chloe was little and I was currently in the throes of raising my third anxious toddler, so the topic seemed appropriate.

I submitted a proposal, sent it to a publisher, and totally forgot about it until I received a letter a few months later. They loved the idea and wanted to move forward with the book. I was dumbfounded. I had actually completely forgotten that I had submitted the proposal.

The next few months were full of intense writing and second-guessing, but eventually the book was done. I thought that was that. But then I got an email from the publisher outlining how the author should market their book. I hadn't thought about marketing. I naively thought that was something they would do. *I have to market this book? How do I do that?*

As I do with everything else in my life, I poured my whole self into learning everything I could about marketing. I printed out the email with their list of to-dos and got right to business. I googled, "What is a platform?" Because apparently that's what I needed. By the time I was done I had a website called AnxiousToddlers.com. I chose that domain based on my newfound understanding of search engine optimization and key word ranking. I was knee deep in uncharted territory and I was just getting started.

Within a few months, I was up to my ears in mommy blogging. I had a Facebook page and a Pinterest account, and I was guest blogging for *Huffington Post*, *PsychCentral* and *Scary Mommy*.

I was consumed with this new world and couldn't get enough. I was developing my voice behind the keyboard and people were appreciating it—they were appreciating *me*. It wasn't long before the original purpose of the "platform" started to fade and a new vision began to form.

As I checked my stats for the hundredth time that day I turned to Jimmie and pointed to my iPad, "There is a whole other world out there. This online world is like a new frontier. You can reach so many more people than being in your office working with one person at a time."

He listened as he sat next to me on the couch, my hand busily typing my latest article instead of scratching his back like I usually did.

I grew obsessed with creating my online world. My website grew as I churned out three articles a week on all types of parenting issues. It wasn't long before I grew bored with toddler topics. I was stuck on rinse and repeat, writing articles about potty training and picky eating. I decided to switch gears and wrote about parenting kids of all ages. I thought, *Who cares if my website is anxioustoddlers.com?* I just couldn't do it anymore.

As much as I loved the new voice I was given and the audience who showered me with appreciation, there was a dark side to the online world. It was a world that was allowed to berate you, humiliate you and hide behind their keyboard. A world where mommy bloggers gossiped about each other and formed online cliques. A world that my Paro was chomping at the bit wanting to taste.

Instead of hiding in my online cave, I continued to venture out into the World Wide Web. I continued to slay online dragons. Unlike in-person interactions, I was able to retreat and lick my wounds before hitting the keyboard and responding to hateful comments.

I had been a virtual punching bag for mommy-anger-gone-wild until I finally learned I didn't have to respond. I didn't have to defend the virtues of what I said, and frankly it didn't matter. Like an anthropologist studying the behaviors of a long-lost tribe, I examined and mastered the inner workings of the online world. The cyber bullying, the feeding frenzy around hate, the desire to watch a virtual fight. I wanted no part of it.

I killed people with love and respect and when that didn't work, I found the delete button. Hurtful, insidious comments didn't have to live on in the work I offered the world. I cocooned myself as much as I could, but I knew I had to grow elephant skin.

Still, as much as you may want to hide, people will find you. They will hunt you down just to knock you off your feet. It became impossible to protect myself completely. I took off the options for comments on my website, because as my traffic grew, so did the comments. One negative comment in a sea of praise could cause my stomach to churn and make me feel as if I was swimming under water for days.

I was real, honest and blunt in my writing. I shared my life and my vulnerabilities. I didn't know how to be any other way. I was as transparent as Scotch tape. For the most part, people applauded my authenticity; they appreciated a therapist who didn't sugarcoat parenting, a parent who was in the trenches with them. But there were always a few who wanted to make you as miserable as they were. Like a drug-sniffing dog, they could smell insecurity a mile away and once they picked up your scent, they wouldn't let go.

At the same time, I finally came to realization that I *did* have social anxiety. I noticed my continual fear of being judged or criticized. I connected the dots in my repeated social patterns. Being online was social anxiety boot camp. I placed myself firmly in the public's eye, naked and exposed, and I did it repeatedly every single day.

Like a vaccine that injects you with the very thing you don't want to get, I started to develop some immunity from it all. I was able to ward off the negative feelings that usually followed hurtful comments. I started to shrug off the corrections on how I mispronounced a word or how I made a glaring spelling mistake. I beat them to the punch, openly and publicly accepting all my faults. I embraced my mistakes and asked others to do the same. Monkey see, monkey do.

It took me a few years, but I was able to trade in my thin, translucent skin and replace it with a rugged, almost impenetrable new one. I had graduated boot camp and survived mostly unscathed, gaining strength and stamina to face the world, even the ugly underbelly.

After a while, I felt as if I was drowning in a sea of Pinterest-perfect parenting tips. I felt as if I was on a hamster wheel, creating more and more content, with little impact or depth.

My children, Chloe, Xander and Alex, were all struggling with some form of anxiety or OCD. I was in my own vicious battle with what I finally knew was social anxiety and my two daughters were trying to slay the beast as well.

I wanted to talk about real things and help with real struggles. I had changed my private practice to focus purely on anxiety and OCD many years before, so I decided I would pivot my online work to concentrate solely on that as well. It was risky since I already had a following, but producing more cardboard for the world to consume just wasn't lighting me up.

Around the same time, I wrote a second book, *Anxiety Sucks: A Teen Survival Guide*, only this time I self-published it. I also created my first online course, How to Teach Kids to Crush Anxiety, and I started a podcast, *The AT Parenting Survival Podcast*. And just because I don't know how to do anything half-assed, I created a YouTube channel called *Ask the Child Therapist*. A bit overkill, to say the least.

I stopped writing and I started talking. The mic was my new keyboard and I quickly fell in love with it. I could share my intimate thoughts and feelings and be as raw as I wanted. I could teach other parents how to raise kids with anxiety or OCD through the lens of my own struggles and my own messy imperfection. I could talk to people on my YouTube channel and give them direct help.

I soaked up the satisfaction that I was making a difference. Hateful comments and emails were quickly replaced with messages of gratitude and appreciation. The lack of services, support and information for parents raising kids with anxiety or OCD became glaringly obvious. Parents wanted to hear from a real person, not a therapist who was teaching them a move from their graduate school playbook. The fact that my hands were dirty with this mess too made my work more meaningful. I didn't just practice this stuff, I was living it as well.

* * *

The accolades I received online drowned out the trickle of negativity that still managed to ooze in. My self-confidence and ability to believe in myself continued to grow. The inoculation I got by putting myself in a position to be judged had been well worth it. I was no longer made of glass, worried I was about to be shattered.

But even with all that, I was still riding along with training wheels. Podcasts were recorded in my pajamas and were edited to perfection. YouTube videos were filtered, manipulated and spliced. I avoided doing anything live, especially Facebook Lives. Those two words sent a shiver down my spine.

"Nope. I'll never do one," I said to a blogging acquaintance. "That is like walking naked on stage and I have zero interest in ever doing it."

Facebook Lives were new at the time, and everyone was flocking to them as if they were the latest fashion craze. "You must go live," I was told by one blogger. "That's really the only way you'll ever engage people on Facebook." I'd roll my eyes, hoping she wasn't right.

I spent time watching other people do Facebook Lives, as if it was a spectator sport. It was like watching acrobats fly through the air at a cheap circus, wondering if they'd make it to the other side. I would stare at my iPad, my gaze transfixed on the train wreck as I wondered, *Does she know the cameras are on? Why is she just staring at the screen and fixing her hair?*

What was worse were the people who jumped off the cliff and crashed to the bottom. *What's that on her neck. A rash, a birthmark? Oh no, it's creeping up her face. She is being swallowed by a sea of red.* It was hard to watch. *Just end it please! This is torture to watch!*

Nope, not for me.

But what I wouldn't do for myself, I would be peer pressured into doing for someone else. That's how I worked. I aimed to please and looked for social acceptance under every nook and cranny. I could see my mom, hands on her hips, eyes narrowing asking, "If they jumped off the Empire State Building would you follow?" The answer apparently is yes, yes I would. Especially if it meant I would gain their approval.

I sat watching the mom blogger, Sally, give us directions on my iPad. We were all promoting her new online course, for a commission. "You all really need to be doing Facebook Lives today. It will make a huge difference." I watched her Facebook Live as she told us to do Facebook Lives; it was like one of those pictures of a mirror reflecting a mirror inside a mirror. "You aren't doing all you can if you aren't talking directly to your audience. They need to know about this and it's your job to tell them. You are doing them a disservice to hold back this information." Sally was a good saleswoman. She should have been a used car salesman. I'd buy a 1970s' Ford Fairmont from her any day.

I was knee deep in the blogging world and I was in the middle of her launch. In the last few years, I had learned what a runway, launch and affiliate partnership meant. I had developed a vocabulary of acronyms such as SEO (search engine optimization), CPL (cost per lead), and ROI (return on investment). It was a whole underworld culture, and it had its own rules that I was drowning in.

She messaged me a few hours later. "Hey friend, are you going to do a Facebook Live?"

I felt annoyed and anxious as I typed back, "I don't think so, Facebook Lives make me nervous." *Please leave me alone.*

No such luck. The three dots blinked at me and then a message popped up.

"I know it's hard. I get nervous too, but your people *need* you. Your work is so important and your audience values what you say." She was good and I desperately wanted her approval. She was a much bigger blogger than me and I had been excited I was invited into the "cool kids club" to promote her latest course.

"I know you can do this, Natasha. I have seen your work," she continued as she lathered on the praise and pressure. She was kryptonite and my powers to resist were quickly fading.

I paused and then typed, "Well, I guess I can try." I didn't want to disappoint her and besides, she seemed to put a lot of value in what I could bring to the launch.

"Great!" she quickly typed back and with that she was suddenly gone. I stared at the silent screen. *What just happened?*

It would be years before I realized I didn't have a special bond or internet friendship with Sally. She didn't love me or my work and think I was special. I was a means to an end. I was a conduit to growing a bank account and feeding her success. It would take me years in this mom-eat-mom world to realize where I stood and where I didn't want to stand. It would take me years to realize when someone was using me, hiding behind the veil of friendship to wiggle their way in.

I sat in my bedroom, where the light from the window was the most flattering. My iPad sat on the small table next to me, like a loaded gun waiting to start the chaos.

I took a deep breath. *What the hell?* I thought. *Why on earth am I doing this? This isn't worth it.* But I didn't want to disappoint Sally. After all, she told me that I was one of her favorite bloggers and that I would go far.

There were so many things I didn't like about Facebook Lives. For example, the small number in the corner that told you how many people were bothering to watch you. If there weren't very many, it was like a virtual rejection. People were seeing your face and scroll-rejecting you. If there were too many, it felt as if people were stopping to watch a traffic accident, sick and voyeuristic, waiting for you to fail.

Then there was the business of the numbers. As you talk you see your views dropping, another one down, another one down, another one bites the dust. How can people focus when there is literally a rejection number in the corner of the screen?

And then there are the comments and the emojis. What if someone says something rude? What if someone asks a question that I don't know the answer to? What if someone gets angry and starts insulting me? Also, how on earth am I supposed to go on when I see an angry emoji face float up over my head? Did I upset someone? Did I say something controversial? Or did they just have big fingers and press the wrong reaction?

Doing a Facebook Live was like juggling while staring straight ahead, trying to string a coherent sentence together. It was a feat that seemed beyond impossible for someone who is as sensitive as I am.

I had been to the bathroom twice to empty out my nerves, and my stomach still screamed for more. Paro was eating popcorn and had a front row seat to the disaster. He had a megaphone in his hand and was shouting, *Best day ever! Go on, make a fool out of yourself. Don't worry, we'll watch the replay together.*

Nothing was going to get better, not my stomach, not Paro, and not my nerves. I decided it was show time and hit the button and watched the red "LIVE" button appear next to the number 0. It was like going on a rollercoaster and then changing your mind when you got to the very top. There was no turning back.

The irony is that I usually do well under pressure. I wear a facade of confidence and calm to hide my death grip and knotted stomach. And here I was in my calm facade. "Well hello there, this is Natasha," I began, feeling the rollercoaster death drop. "For those of you who don't know me, I am a child therapist..." Words started to fly out of me, my eyes darting to the number in the left-hand corner: 3 then 5 then 7, then back to 5.

I continued to talk.

"So, the other day my daughter was struggling with..." I was moving into one of my stories. I felt at home when I was revealing the inner workings of my own parenting and my own struggles. The more real I was, the more at home I started to feel.

The little eye in the corner read 10 then 9 then 11. I was getting dizzy from the feedback. I finished up my story, talked about Sally's program, and said my goodbyes.

I put the weapon back on the table and surveyed the damage. Was I bleeding? Was it a superficial wound? Would I recover?

Like a moth to a flame, I grabbed my iPad and looked at the comments. Only a few. "Nice to see you," one said. "Love her program!" another commented. "My daughter does the same thing," the last one wrote.

My hands were visibly shaking. *Well, that was pure unadulterated torture.*

I sat next to my window waiting for the shaking to stop when a message popped on my screen. It was Sally. Like a drug dealer excited that I had taken my first free hit she wrote, "Great Live! I knew you could do it. Try to do one every day this week."

Chapter 19
Now

It had been several months since I decided to push myself into severe discomfort and go to the IOCDF conference. My mind and gut had recovered, but I knew I had more work to do. Afterall, I had already done these challenges in the past. I had gone to trainings with Jimmie by my side. Where had all my progress gone? Why did it feel as if I was starting from scratch?

So, when I got an email from an entrepreneurial program I was part of about an in-person event, my hand hovered and paused before I hit delete. *You know, we could go?* Natasha Version 2.0 piped in.

Nah, I'm good, I argued back. *Haven't we had enough walking on hot coals for one year?*

But she had her argument locked and loaded. *Yeah, but you went with your security blanket. You had Jimmie. You had your little human shields. That was the play-offs. You need a Super Bowl. Also, you have done a lot of this work before and lost all your progress. You have to claw your way back. We don't want anything like a stupid Facebook post about you to ever take that much power away from you again.*

I had stopped arguing too much with her. She knew what she was doing, and, annoyingly, she had a good point. *You have to go to this. You can't waste this experience. Besides, this is Paro holding you back. You know you have to do the opposite of anything Paro tells you, right?*

Ugh. I hated it when she was right. I frantically messaged anyone I knew in the online world who was in the same program, all two of them. Neither of them were able to go.

Natasha Version 2.0 had already made up her mind, she was RSVPing and booking the flight.

All done! she whispered. Her fingers flew to Facebook and started scrolling through the program's private Facebook group. I knew what she was doing, and I begged for her to stop.

Yup, there's one! she said as she typed. "I need a roommate too! Do you want to share a room?"

I couldn't stop this train wreck. My alter ego was on full speed ahead and before the night was over, I was not only going, but I was rooming with a stranger. What had I done?

Later that night, as I sheepishly looked at my email with my flight confirmation, I asked Jimmie, "Do you mind if I go to a live event in California?"

He looked up from his iPad as he lay on the couch. "No, do what you need to do," he said and then paused before continuing. "Where in California? Maybe I can take the kids to Disney while you're at the conference?" He was used to a wife who couldn't walk around the block by herself, let alone fly to another state.

I bit my bottom lip. "Actually, I think I'll go to this one by myself if you don't mind. It will be good for my social anxiety.

I need a bigger challenge." I looked over at him to see if he would be offended. He continued to play word search on his iPad, his usual poker face revealing nothing.

A few minutes later he picked up his work phone to scroll through his calendar. "Okay, when is it?"

I suddenly realized he would have to do kid duty and I felt a pang of guilt. I had been so focused on challenging myself, I had forgotten he'd have to be alone with the kids. He didn't look thrilled, but he didn't say anything.

"Okay, I'll ask for the time off tomorrow," he said as he clipped his work phone back on to his belt. I put my iPad down, got up and squeezed myself between the couch and his back, "You're the best," I said, wrapping my arms around him.

For the next few weeks I tried not to think about it. *Back burner it*, I told myself. Unfortunately, time flies when you aren't consumed with worry, and before I knew it, I was messaging a stranger to see where she wanted to meet.

"Do you want to meet at the hotel or the airport?" I typed, hoping she'd say airport. I needed, no I *wanted*, a surrogate Jimmie. I had never taken an Uber alone before and the idea of navigating the app, spotting a stranger's car and carrying on a conversation for the whole ten miles seemed more than I wanted to do.

"I think I am going to take the airport shuttle to the hotel," she wrote back, throwing me a curve ball.

Paro piped right in. *Ooh, the airport shuttle. What if you can't find it? What if you are left stranded at the airport for hours and hours?*

I swallowed hard and typed again, "Or we can meet up and take an Uber together?" *Ugh, can you sound any more clingy?*

Thankfully she agreed, and Paro quieted down.

When I arrived in California I was feeling cautiously brave and empowered. Natasha Version 2.0 was cheerleading the entire way. *Look at you go! Walking into a tornado of fear with such bravery!* It felt good to hear some positive inner dialogue going on for once. It also felt good that Paro was speechless.

It was easy to spot Ellen in the small regional airport. It also helped that I had cyber-stalked her and knew exactly what she looked like. I saw her curly gray hair and glasses from across the baggage carousel and I headed over. She was appropriately friendly, and I felt at ease. We went on the hunt to get an Uber, but then decided it would be easier to just find the hotel shuttle. We rode up the escalator and found the sign that said "Hotel Shuttles." I noted to myself that Paro often made a mountain out of a molehill. *I could have found it on my own!*

As we headed into the hotel I started to feel jittery. It's so hard to shake off the you-are-on-stage-and-everyone-is-watching-you feeling. We got into our room and I plopped my bag on the crisp, white duvet and then I saw it. Hanging from the bathroom frame was not a door, but one of those sliding contraptions. I tried not to show my complete panic as I casually walked over. No lock and a half-inch gap on both sides. *Fuck. Can I hold my poop for three days? I guess we'll find out.*

I started to wonder if rooming with a stranger was a bad idea? Like taking a big bite of a fruity chew only to realize you are going to choke if you swallow it all. As I sat on the bed pondering what I had got myself into she said, "You want to go find the restaurant?"

"Sure," I said, and flashed a tight smile.

Five minutes into dinner I realized we were not a match made in heaven. I felt as if I was on a bad blind date with no exit strategy. She was as quiet as me—no, even quieter. Her eyes darted around the restaurant and beyond, into the hotel lobby. *Is she bored of me? Does she wish that she could be over there, with those people, drinking and being loud? Or is she nervous? Does she have social anxiety?*

As she ate her French fries and stared past me, I did a full assessment of her possible diagnoses. I settled on no diagnosis, most likely an introvert. I then added possible social anxiety disorder, but I was leaning towards ruling it out, as she looked too comfortable.

Back in the room, I spent the evening working on my iPad as she buried her head in a book. I doubled down on my initial diagnostic impressions and officially ruled out social anxiety disorder. She was way too casual and quiet to be my social anxiety soul sister.

The next morning, Ellen was up bright and early. "I'm going to head down and get some coffee," she said, pulling her backpack over her shoulders. Normally this would have sent waves of panic through my body. I would have thrown on some pants, looked desperate and hurried to Velcro myself to her for the day. "Wait for me, I'll come too..." I would have said, trying to hide my desperation.

But this was the new me and if last night was any indicator, I was pretty sure I didn't want to ride on those particular coattails anyway. She wanted to ride solo.

I couldn't help but feel abandoned though. I thought that one of the upsides of rooming with a stranger was the built-in security blanket she would provide. She was supposed to be a warm body to protect me from the sea of strangers waiting downstairs. "Okay, I'll see you down there," I said as I watched my surrogate Jimmie abandon her post.

I sat alone on the bed. *What have I done?* This wasn't a Super Bowl challenge, it was a gladiator challenge, a battle to the death, and I wasn't confident which side would win.

I got dressed and headed down to the lobby. Natasha Version 2.0 was working overtime. *You've got this. Who cares what people think. Just go down there and enjoy the conference. You're winning for just being here, everything else you do is gravy.*

As I got into the elevator I reminded myself that my challenge wasn't to make friends, it was to be okay with who I am, to be okay with *how* I am. I'm quiet and introverted, that wasn't the problem. The problem was the meaning and judgment I placed on my behavior. It was the paranoia and self-consciousness that consumed me and shut me down, not my quiet demeanor.

I was like Rocky before a fight, all amped up and ready to go—that is, until the elevator door opened, and I saw hundreds of people swarming around the lobby. It felt like the harsh sting of cold air after you leave a warm car, and all my positive self-talk seeped out of me. But there was no turning back.

I saw a growing line starting to form at the hotel Starbucks. I joined the herd of caffeine junkies. It was something to do, a prop to hold. I no longer drank coffee—irritable bowel syndrome robbed me of that and the dignity to poop on my terms, but a warm cup of confidence sounded delicious.

"Kelly! Oh my God, so good to see you. This is my friend

Mark." A reunion was happening in front of me, new friendships were being made.

I eavesdropped on the conversation behind me. I was drowning in the sea of exclusion. Paro quickly went to work. *Everyone has already made friends. Look around you at all the people connecting and socializing. You are just standing here alone, like a social reject, again. You've brought us to your worst nightmare.*

I itched to get my phone out to look busy, but then I reconsidered. *No, I'm fine. I can do this. I can stand here in the sea of socialization. Why do I care? Who are these people anyway? Besides, no one is hyper-focusing on me, wondering why I am standing here by myself. Nobody gives a shit, and neither should I.*

I grabbed my tea and wrapped both my hands around the cup. The warmth felt good against my cold, clammy hands. I nudged my feet to move in the direction of the hall. I walked alone in the crowd of people who had already found belonging. The hall was packed and from the corner of my eye I could see a woman standing with her coffee watching the crowd.

As I walked past her, she started to walk with me.

At first I didn't realize she was talking to me.

"I'm Natasha, but people call me Sophia," she started in, as if we had been in the middle of a conversation I wasn't privy to.

I didn't know where she came from, but I wanted to hug her. She was like the arrival of an aircraft after you think no one saw your smoke signals. I tried to remain casual. "Really? That's so weird. My name is Natasha too," I said, both of us laughing, me more from nerves. Her energy was light and freeing. She was shorter than me, but her confidence and personality towered above us both.

We entered the hotel ballroom and found our seats among the packed crowd. The room was dim, the empty stage lit by bright lights. Sophia was real and raw and didn't hold back. I found her refreshing. We spoke in half shouts above the noise until the conference began.

The day flew by and I was riding on the fumes of excitement and relief. During our break, Sophia asked if I wanted to go to lunch. I was so thankful that I wouldn't have to eat alone.

When we returned to the conference, Sophia started conversations with people all around us. I had found the most perfect coattail to ride, or rather it had found me.

"What type of work do you do?" she asked a girl sitting next to us. "I'm Sophia and this is Natasha," she would add.

I was meeting so many people, but more importantly I was knee deep in training. This conference was as much about growing my online business as it was about my social anxiety. This trip was supposed to be the Super Bowl of challenges, and I'd just found my most valuable player. Her ability to casually approach people and start conversations was admirable.

Later, we were sitting alone as the crowd poured out. "You make talking to new people seem so easy. I wish I was like that."

She smiled and laughed, "I'm not always like that. I can be quieter and more reserved too."

But what she didn't realize is that she could effortlessly switch between the two. She could downshift when she wanted, but it was *her* choice.

* * *

The next day I felt more emboldened and empowered than I had the day before. Ellen left to go downstairs early again, and I celebrated by going to the bathroom in solitude.

As I pushed the L button and descended, I had no trembles and no need for Rocky-themed music. There was no sensation of being thrown off a 20-story building or the realization halfway down that I'd forgotten a parachute. No, I was hang-gliding all the way to the lobby. The best part was that it was only partly due to the security Sophia had brought to me the day before.

Natasha Version 1.0 would have made arrangements to meet up in the lobby. But Natasha Version 2.0 didn't do that. This was the Super Bowl, not some practice. There would be no security nets, no training wheels, no human shields to soften the struggle. This was about being as vulnerable as possible and sitting in the discomfort it would inevitably bring. It was about pushing my limits to prove that I could survive. It wasn't about finding shortcuts and loopholes. It wasn't about making friends and developing long-term friendships. It was about crushing Paro, one incredibly awkward, uncomfortable moment at a time.

I walked among the crowds who gathered in the halls. Paro remained quiet, huddled in the darkest corner. I felt no self-consciousness, no spotlight following my every move, no stage where everyone was staring at me, mocking me. I felt free in a sea of people for the first time in my life. It was as if someone had removed a 500-pound brick from my back that I hadn't even realized I was carrying.

I went to the coffee and tea stand and poured myself some

herbal tea. The doors to the large ballroom opened. I saw no sign of Sophia. Normally this would throw me into panic overdrive. I would feel naked and exposed.

I found a scattering of empty seats and sat down, taking another sip of my hot tea, watching people talk all around me. I was uncomfortable, but it was manageable. The old Natasha would have been scanning the crowd for her designated human security blanket while listening to Paro berate her for being a loser and sitting alone.

I surveyed the crowd, this time not to highlight all the successful social interactions I was not a part of, but rather to find someone who was sitting alone as well. I saw a woman a few aisles up who was sitting by herself. I felt a new challenge whispering in my ear, nudging me to act. *Get up and go introduce yourself. We didn't come here to play it safe. What's the worst thing that could happen? That she doesn't want to be chatty?* I felt as if I was at a point where I could handle that. Challenges weren't supposed to be about proving you could be successful, they were about proving you could handle the results regardless of how they turn out.

I got up and walked down the aisle. The woman was wearing a bright red sweater and her salt and pepper hair was pulled back. She was in a row of empty seats, but I pointed to the seat next to her and said, "Is anyone sitting here?"

She looked up, possibly lost in thought and said, "What?"

I nervously bit my cheek, but tried again, "Is anyone sitting here?"

"Oh, no, go ahead," she said, pointing to the seat. I sat down and she continued to look forward. She was not making this challenge easy, but I was all in at this point. I tapped my fingers on the chair and then pulled the trigger. "Hey, I'm Natasha," I said, trying not to sound too stilted or weird.

Her unfriendly gaze broke into a smile and she said, "I'm Claire, nice to meet you."

From there the questions flowed easily out of my mouth. I never had a problem having a conversation; it was starting one that always held me back. As we chatted, people in the row in front of us started to turn around and talk as well. It felt good. It was like the first touchdown of the Super Bowl.

Sophia showed up a few minutes later. It was nice to have someone seek me out. I had accepted the possibility that she would move on, find another person to bond with, and my connection with her would be over. I was trying to shift my thinking and move to acceptance mode. *What will be, will be.* That's hard for an anxious person—especially one who wants to guarantee her comfort and avoid being alone.

"Hey, lady!" Sophia said, her face breaking into a beautiful broad smile. We scooted our feet in as she sat down next to us.

"This is Claire," I said, feeling like a child showing her mom that she rode her bike alone for the first time. Sophia didn't miss a beat. She was best friends with the entire row before the conference even started. I soaked up her energy and social ease like a student thirsty for mastery.

Shortly before the conference began, a woman with curly black hair came to our aisle and scooted next to Claire. They smiled at each other. "This is Jan," Claire said, introducing the two of us. "We met at another conference," she explained.

Jan jumped right into the conversation as if we were all long-lost friends. *How do these people do this with such ease?*

The lights came down and a speaker came on stage.

I thought about the monumental shift that was happening. My body filled with warmth and self-compassion. Natasha Version 2.0 was at the podium giving a victory speech in my head.

* * *

At a break, we all went to the lobby to stretch our legs and go to the bathroom. Sophia and I got in the bathroom line. Within seconds she was already deep in conversation with the girl next to us. They chatted like long-lost friends. "That's so interesting. I want to do that type of work too. Do you coach only women?"

I listened to them talk as we inched one more step to the stalls. Normally I would feel possessive when my newly identified human shield was talking to someone else. It would feel like a threat. I hung on to my social anxiety security blankets like a newborn baby clings to its mother.

Paro would normally whisper in my ear, *She thinks you are boring. She is desperate to try and talk to someone else. Look how you are just standing here, not talking. They must think you are so weird. Say something, do something!*

But this time my mind was pleasantly silent. All I could hear were the sounds of flushing and laughter. I felt no threat. I wasn't clinging on to Sophia for dear life. She was not my raft in a dark and choppy sea. I was sailing on my own.

After I went to the bathroom, I washed my hands and looked around. Sophia was nowhere in sight. *Is she still in the bathroom? Did she leave and go back to her seat?* I was frustrated that social anxiety made every single social interaction so awkward for me. Did other people not worry about this stuff?

I dried my hands and scanned the room again, this time with a bit more desperation. Sophia was still nowhere in sight. Would it be weird for me to just hover in the bathroom and wait for her? There was still a line of people waiting. Would it seem strange to just stand there? Or should I leave and wait for her outside? Would that seem too clingy, too desperate? I didn't want to come off as desperate. But I also didn't want to seem rude. Would it be rude to just leave her and go back to my seat? I knew I wouldn't like it if the person I was with just left me, but I also knew I wasn't like everyone else. *Think, think. What would a normal person do?* My mind drew a blank. No idea. I had never been normal.

I stood there in ambivalence, looking like a child who had lost her mother, when I finally asked myself what would the old Natasha Version 1.0 do? That answer I did know. She would wait. She would cling on to Sophia like a parasite clings on to their host.

I headed for the door and walked through the crowd back to my seat. This wasn't about whether Sophia would be offended or hurt, although I knew she had enough social sophistication to fend for herself. This was about me doing what didn't feel right. It was about choosing discomfort whenever faced with a choice.

A few minutes later Sophia joined us with a warm drink in her hand. "I wonder where we should go for lunch?" she asked as she took a sip of her drink. She probably hadn't even thought twice about the fact that I wasn't there when she came out of the bathroom, people like that never do. I wanted to be like her when I grew up.

* * *

At the lunch break, a group of us headed outside to the line of food trucks. I was looking at how far the line stretched when I noticed a familiar face, sitting alone, legs crossed on a small patch of grass. It was Ellen, my roommate. She was by herself, reading a book.

My heart sank. That was *my* worst fear. I felt guilty and ashamed for having an entourage of people with me as she sat alone. I thought about how hard this must be for her, sitting alone in a crowd full of people. I was about to go up and rescue her from self-isolation and discomfort when I took a second glance. Was I seeing her situation from my point of view? She didn't seem uncomfortable. Her body seemed relaxed as she flipped through the pages of her book. She didn't glance around nervously every few minutes, as I surely would have done. She seemed to be genuinely engrossed in her novel.

My brain flashed back to my brief interactions with her. She was going to take the shuttle by herself, until I basically begged her to wait for me at the airport. She wasn't talkative at dinner but showed no signs of nervousness. She readily left me the first morning to go into a crowd of strangers in the lobby. I had an epiphany! I wasn't staring at a kindred spirit. I was staring at an introvert, an introvert *without* social anxiety. People always confuse the two or meld them together, but it's like comparing apples to oranges.

Yes, I was an introvert. But that was neither here nor there when it came to my social anxiety. Social anxiety was an equal opportunity disorder. It would take you down either way, it didn't care.

Ellen didn't need my rescuing. She was most likely recharging after being bombarded with people all morning. My efforts to "save" her would likely be seen as a disruption, not a welcomed rescue.

I stood in awe. I realized that I didn't want to grow up to be Sophia, I wanted to grow up to be Ellen. Sophia was naturally outgoing. She was a social creature to the core. I was more like Ellen, an introvert through and through. But the insecurities that closed up my throat and deprived me of air prevented me from doing exactly what Ellen was doing right now. The fear of looking pathetic, isolated and rejected kept me from sitting on a small patch of grass, unconcerned about how the world would see me. She was a rockstar.

I stared out the airplane window as we taxied down the runway. I felt lighter, no longer weighed down by the doubt and insecurities. In five short days, my progress had been catapulted ahead, silencing the social anxiety beast. And although I knew Natasha Version 2.0 had been fully uploaded, I was no longer naive. I knew that social anxiety would always be with me, like an unwanted wart that threatened to grow. I'd always have to keep an eye on it.

Chapter 20
Then

Cavedale Drive

In the early days of my online career, I had finally identified Paro and made my first attempt to rid myself of him. He was now on the run, like a lost warrior trying to make it back to his hiding spot. But now that I had finally identified my enemy, I wasn't about to let him get away.

I felt like a cardiologist who had lived their life treating everyone else's heart condition, while ignoring their own diseased heart. How could I have missed that I had social anxiety? It had been debilitating me my whole life and yet only when I started to grow my self-worth did I see Paro standing there behind the curtain.

How would I help a person with social anxiety in my practice? What type of treatment would I offer? I knew it was time to get systematic and strategic. I couldn't just stay on the defense, warding off Paro whenever he decided to attack. I had to start playing offense. I had to start pursuing him.

I grabbed a piece of paper from the desk in my office and started to brainstorm, just as I would instruct someone in therapy to do. I thought about situations that fed Paro and grew him bigger. I thought about situations that made me squirm and numbered them 1 to 10, 1 being no big deal, 10 being those where I would rather crawl under a rock and die.

- Go to the mailbox at the end of my street alone. 4
- Walk through the reception area of the gym and risk being greeted by the overly talkative receptionist, instead of doing my usual ninja move and using the back door. 5
- Start a conversation with the cashier while checking my groceries out. 6
- Go to a children's birthday party without Jimmie. 7
- Go to a training where I don't know anyone. 10
- Go to a training out of state, alone, where I don't know anyone. 11+

As if talking to a client, I told myself that I was now supposed to start working through this list. It didn't have to be in order, and I could do other scary challenges as they popped up, but this list needed to eventually get done. It was like a reverse bucket list, which brought fear and nausea instead of joy and excitement, but I vowed to follow through.

I stood as she scanned our food. Beep. Beep. Beep. Walmart was crowded and she looked exhausted. In the corner of the cash register I saw a crocheted cover that was keeping her water bottle from sweating. I wondered if she had made it herself. Ask her. You must ask her something. I volleyed back excuses.

She's tired, she doesn't want someone to force her to talk. I'll do it, just not today.

But a deal is a deal and I promised myself that I was all in. Before I could give doubt any more attention, I heard myself blurt out, "I like your water bottle cover. Did you make that?"

The lines on her face softened and the pace of her scanning slowed just a bit. "Yes, I love crocheting. I made this too," she said, pointing to a key chain.

"That's cool," I said, not really knowing what to say. But with that simple question, I had opened the floodgates of conversation, letting her know that she was seen and that she would be heard.

"I also make these cute beds for my cats. They love them. It looks like you have a cat," she said as she scanned my cat food. "What kind do you have?"

I told her about our two rag doll cats that are bigger than some small dogs. Her face lit up as she started another story, but I had paid, and it was time to move on.

Well, that wasn't hard. Why did that initially feel like free-falling off a cliff? I knew intellectually that this was the point—to call your anxiety's bluff, to accept the outcome no matter what happens, to sit with discomfort. But minutes before, it had seemed like such a big mountain to climb. Now looking back, I realized it was just a small hill.

After that first challenge, it was game on. Paro had been calling the shots my entire life and I was ready to finally fight back.

I climbed the last few stairs of the community center and turned to the left, not avoiding the social minefields of the gym.

"Hey lady, how's it going today?" the receptionist said before I even made it completely inside.

"Going well, how about you?"

"Saw your article this month. Just finished reading it in fact," she held it up and waved it back and forth, just in case I didn't believe her.

I winced. "Oh, cool," I uttered, trying to continue past her desk.

"No kids today?" she asked, forcing me to slow down.

"Nope, they're all at school." I smiled, eyeing the entrance to the gym.

"They're back already. Gosh, summer ends so fast these days."

"Yup. It does." I said, hoping we were done.

"Well, have a good workout."

"You too," I said.

I walked towards the gym and berated myself. You too. *You too?* God, I hated when I did that. I quickly surveyed the room. Two men in the corner lifting weights, three women on treadmills. The room was small and I felt claustrophobic and conspicuous. Gyms always did that to me. I felt permanently on display. It was enough to make me not want to go—that and of course the actual idea of exercise.

I strategically picked an elliptical machine that was far enough from the men lifting weights but not too close to the women on the treadmills. I plopped my water bottle in the holder and put my headphones on self-consciously as I looked around the room.

A podcast distracted me, and I was quickly in a rhythm. I hopped off the machine and made my way to the wipes. I had read all the rules, many times over.

1. Wipe down all equipment when you are done.
2. Wear proper gym attire. No spaghetti straps.
3. Be considerate, don't stay on machines longer than 30 minutes if someone is waiting.

Number 2 had ruined an entire workout the year before. What constituted spaghetti straps? The ones I was sporting were more like fettuccine straps. Was fettuccine okay? I spent the entire workout comparing the thickness of my straps to those around me. I survived that day but never wore a tank top again. Better to not risk it, I had thought.

I hopped off the elliptical and went to the yoga balls to do some back stretches and sit-ups. As I lifted myself up I heard an annoying screeching sound from one of the machines. Like clockwork every five seconds I heard it again, EEEK 1-2-3-4-5, EEEK 1-2-3-4-5, EEEK. I wanted to punch the person making the noise. *Get off the machine,* I wanted to shout. Noises irritated me.

I finished my sit-ups as the room fell silent once again, thank God. I wiped down the yoga ball and went on to the thigh weights. I put both my feet on the bar and pushed my knees out, feeling the burn through both my legs, and that's when I heard it, that all too familiar EEEK sound. *Shit,* I thought. *Just my luck.* I looked next to me and saw the other machine with the same thigh weights available. I started to get up to switch machines when I felt an annoying tug. *Are you getting up to avoid embarrassment?* I quickly argued back. *But anyone would get up. It's annoying. It would annoy other people.* Ugh. Checkmate. *Yes, exactly.*

I sat back down like a child who is told they cannot leave the dinner table, and I reluctantly did another rep. EEEK, the machine shouted. It felt ten times louder now that I was making the noise. My face heated up and my eyes darted around. *I can't do it,* I pleaded with myself. I'm literally going to get punched in the face. I started to negotiate. *How about five reps? That's better than nothing.* But I was merciless and there would be no negotiating. *No. You normally do 25. Anything less would be cheating.*

I pushed my knees out again. EEEK, the machine laughed back at me. This was legitimately obnoxious and my quick survey around the room told me everyone agreed. I looked down and held my breath. EEEK; 23 more to go. I stopped looking around. I didn't need to survey the crowd to know how my behavior was being received. I had to accept the discomfort. I had to accept the fact that I might be inviting confrontation and that even if I did, I could survive it.

EEEK 1-2-3-4-5, EEEK 1-2-3-4-5, I continued. I counted every painful repetition, my knees jetting out, over and over again. When I was done, I didn't want to look up. I walked over to get a wipe with my eyes down. Avoidance wasn't allowed, so I forced myself to lift up my head. The monotony of the room surprised me. The men in the corner were continuing to lift their weights. The women continued to rhythmically stride on the treadmills. I was in my own personal hell, and no one was the wiser.

After my workout, I pushed open the door to the back stairs—the stairs I normally used to sneak in and avoid the chatty receptionist. The cool air felt good against my sweaty skin. I felt alive. Every challenge I took to crush social anxiety gave me a little piece of myself back.

* * *

I sat on the couch scrolling through my emails. An email from the International OCD Foundation caught my eye. It was an email about an upcoming training. The Behavior Therapy Training Institute (BTTI) was having a pediatric version of their training. I had taken the regular BTTI training course and was on the waiting list to take the pediatric one.

I thought back to the BTTI course I had attended. Jimmie and the kids had gone with me. There wasn't even a thought that I would go by myself. We packed up the family and they went to Disneyland while I sat through days of OCD training. Their presence spared me the stress of being alone. Even with them there, I still remember feeling self-conscious and overwhelmed.

I was gaining momentum in my challenges. I had climbed my exposure ladder just as I had kids do in my practice, and I had made Paro squirm. I was at the top, but I knew there were still insecurities buried under the dirt, like a seed waiting for the right mixture of sun and water to sprout again.

The last thing on my challenge ladder was to attend an out-of-state conference all by myself. This would be a good opportunity to check that box and finish my list.

I was flooded with images of what would come. Me trying to navigate flying alone. The airport, the rental car, driving around a new city trying to find my way. But that would just be the beginning. Then there would be the groups of therapists whispering, talking, laughing. Strangers. People who I didn't know, bonding and reminiscing about something I wasn't a part of and never would be.

My body started to feel sticky under my clothes. *Well, that's a done deal. That has to happen.* I forced my hands to scroll to the registration page.

I repositioned my phone in the rental car and typed the address to the hotel. *You're fine.* I put the car in reverse and took a deep breath. *Just drive.* Wisconsin was full of open space and grassy fields. I easily found my way to the highway and eventually to the hotel. I was thankful for the paint-by-numbers situation; God knows I needed it.

I heaved my heavy bag out of the trunk. It was a naked feeling, being alone. I thought I was a fiercely independent person, but the reality smacked me in the face. I had been in the passenger seat of life for as long as I could remember, and apparently I didn't know how to drive.

When I got into my room I got out my iPad and looked at the training schedule once more. I pulled up a map and looked at how far the hospital was from where I was staying. Every minute detail needed to be organized and arranged in my head to stop the anxious rumblings in my stomach.

I set my phone alarm and lay back on the bed going over

the next day. *It's fine*, I reassured myself. *You'll get through this like you've got through everything else.*

* * *

Rogers Memorial Hospital was more like a college campus than a treatment center. I wound my way through the curvy roads trying to find where I was supposed to park. I thought I had left early enough, but I was suddenly feeling crunched for time. I hated to be rushed. It felt like a pressure cooker with no release valve.

"Your name," the dark-haired woman said, sitting at a table full of name tags looking bored.

"Natasha Daniels." I half-smiled and pointed to my upside-down name tag on the table.

"Here you go," she said.

I aimlessly walked down the hall and found the room. It was already mostly full and smelled of freshly brewed coffee. Groups of two and three sat together. I automatically scanned the room for a spot that had no one around it. Old habits die hard.

I found a table that seemed relatively empty and plopped down. I awkwardly smiled at the girl two seats away, as I hung my purse on the chair. She just stared back.

Ignoring her unfriendliness, I whispered in a conspiratorial tone, "Where did you get the coffee?"

She half smiled and in a hushed tone said, "In the room across the hall. But there wasn't much left." Nothing like a coffee addiction to bring people together.

I got some coffee and then returned to my seat as the

training was just getting started. All my thoughts and insecurities were paused as I immersed myself in the world of OCD. For the first time, I felt grateful I had decided to come to the training. I had been so consumed with fear that I forgot how much I loved learning about this stuff.

I turned over my notebook to continue writing the speaker's last point. The OCD researcher stood at the podium and looked at his watch. I felt a flutter of butterflies in my stomach as I anticipated what he was going to say.

"Now is probably a good time to take a break," he said as he shut his notebook and looked up. The room moaned in agreement.

I wanted to contest. I wanted to shout, "Breaks? who needs those! Those awkward ten minutes where I sit and pretend to look busy while everyone chats and networks. No thanks, we can move on."

But the room was already emptying, and people were getting up to chat and get more coffee. I sat there frozen, like a deer in the middle of a dark, winding road waiting to get hit. I grabbed my paper coffee cup and went into the adjacent room to refill it. It was better than sitting in a half empty room listening to people talk.

Returning, I balanced my coffee cup as I pulled my chair to sit down. I heard two women a few seats away from me starting to talk. "I've worked there for a few years. I like it. How about you?" They were chatting as if they were long-lost friends. Their voices trailed off as my thoughts grew louder. *You can't sit here. That's not the deal. That's not why you are here.*

I scanned the room. Some people were standing, others

were sitting. Laughter exploded from down the hall. I intuitively went to reach for my phone to look busy. My hand hovered over my purse, but then I paused and reprimanded myself. *No. That's avoidance.*

It was torture being your own therapist. I pulled my hand back and placed it in my lap. I hated this. I looked around the table. There was a woman, probably 15 years older than me, sitting a few seats down. She had a sweater draped over her shoulders and was blowing on her hot drink. I stared at her until she felt my gaze. She looked in my direction and I forced a smile. "Have you been to any of these trainings?" I hoped she'd want to strike up a conversation.

"No, this is my first one through the IOCDF. How about you?"

"I went to the general BTTI a little while ago but was really wanting to do this pediatric one."

She smiled and put out her hand. "I'm Sue, by the way," and with that the conversation started to flow. The rest of the break flew by, as these things often do once I find my place in the social chaos. Jumping off the cliff is always the hardest part.

After the last lecture ended, Sue leaned over. "Are you going to the happy hour party later tonight?"

No, I wanted to say. *There would be nothing happy about that hour.* But instead, I put on my fakest smile and said, "Yeah, how about you?"

She scribbled her number on a piece of paper. "How about we go for dinner first and then go together?" That seemed much more doable, and I pounced at the offer. "Perfect! I'll call you tonight and we can meet in the lobby."

It turned out that Sue and I had complementary needs. I needed a human blanket to keep me from social rejection and she needed a chauffeur. It was a match made in heaven. We arrived early to happy hour and had dinner there. We got a quiet booth in the corner. It didn't look as if anyone had arrived yet, so I tried to relax. Sue had a fascinating life, and it was easy to get absorbed in her stories. It was a good distraction. I felt as if I was sitting on a rollercoaster waiting for the ride to start.

We paid our bill and walked to the private room in the back where the happy hour was happening. There were a few people milling around by the bar and a couple of people scattered about, sitting at candlelit tables. We were early.

I sucked in my breath. These are the type of situations I avoided. I instinctively moved closer to Sue. We made our way to the happy hour buffet and grabbed a plate. We had just eaten, but it seemed like the right thing to do. She moved to the bar and ordered wine. At that moment I wished I drank, but I never felt comfortable with alcohol. The loss of control was too threatening.

With wine in hand, Sue walked up to a man standing in the middle of what might have been used as a dance floor. I followed along, desperate to not be abandoned.

"Hey, John, my name is Sue. I met you at the OCD Conference a few years back. I wanted to talk to you about your program..." her words faded as my head swirled.

I'm just standing here like an idiot. Should I leave? Should I try to get involved in the conversation? Neither of them paid any attention to me.

There were two types of people as far as my social anxiety

was concerned. There were social anxiety wingmen who carried me through situations like this and then there were people like Sue, unconcerned about whether I sank or swam. I was sinking, but I wasn't going to stand there and drown.

I smiled at them both and slowly backed away, pretending to want something else at the buffet. My stomach protested as I added a few small hors d'oeuvres to my plate. They hadn't noticed, either of them. Not even a small look in my direction. *You're a big girl, Natasha. This is why you are here. Challenges aren't supposed to be easy. No coattails tonight.*

I looked around feeling like a ship lost at sea with no place to anchor myself. I saw a guy and a girl sitting at one of the small tables. I quickly assessed the situation. My gut said it wasn't romantic. I scanned the room for other options. There were several larger groups of people at tables pushed together. Definitely not an option. There were three tables that were completely empty. An enticing option. The old me would have sat awkwardly at one of the empty tables, sealing my fate for a night of loneliness and discomfort, pretending to look at my cell phone.

I walked up to the small table where the non-couple couple were sitting. "Hey, do you mind if I join you?" I asked, pointing to the empty seat at the table. This wasn't walking off the cliff, this was a swan dive head first.

"Sure," they both said in unison. Relief flooded through me as I pulled out the seat and sat down.

Conversation flowed easily. They hadn't known each other, but they had known mutual people. I felt relieved that my hunch they weren't a couple was right. I looked across the room and saw Sue busily talking to another woman, her wine glass half empty. I refocused my attention on the conversation at my table. I started to feel anchored and empowered. We chatted for the next 20 minutes. Victory music started playing in my head. *Girl! You did it. Not only did you fly all the way here by yourself, but you attended a party and asked to sit with strangers!*

But the record scratched, and the music came to a halt. "I think I'm going to head back to the hotel," the woman said as she yawned.

"Yeah, me too," the guy piped in. *Wait, wait, you can't go. I just imprinted on you. You're my people.*

"Okay, it was nice meeting you guys," I lied, feeling suddenly naked and exposed. They got up and left and I remained at the table alone. I glanced around the room suddenly feeling vulnerable and exhausted. The two large tables behind me were overflowing with people. It seemed too late to try and sit over there. I looked for Sue. She was standing in the center of the room, newly filled wine glass in one hand as she animatedly gesticulated with the other. I had no idea who she was talking to.

I knew I was Sue's ride, but I was done. The old me would have patiently waited for Sue, not wanting to disappoint her or rain on her parade. But one of my goals was to reduce my people pleasing and think about what I wanted, and *I* wanted to go to bed. I stood up having made my decision. I brazenly walked up to Sue and her latest friend. They were deep in conversation. I awkwardly stood there until my presence made everyone uncomfortable. "Sorry to interrupt," I started. "Sue, I'm going to head out. I'm tired."

She barely glanced at me. "It's fine, I'll take an Uber," she said dismissively.

I walked out and felt the fresh breeze on my face. I hadn't realized how suffocated I had felt until I desperately filled my lungs with air. As I drove back through the darkness I over-analyzed the night like only someone with social anxiety can do. Was that a win or a loss? Sometimes it was hard for me to say.

I had gone to the party; that in and of itself was clearly a win. In the past, I would have avoided any unstructured social activity. Also, instead of desperately clinging to my self-appointed social anxiety wingman, I cut my losses early and went at it alone. That was a huge win for me. It went against every grain in my body, but I forced myself to do it anyway. The end of the night was a mixed bag. Was leaving a failure or a success? As an introvert, I have a finite amount of energy to expend, and my battery gets used up twice as fast in social situations. By the end my battery was completely spent. The old me would have put the needs of others over myself. I would never have "abandoned" Sue. I would have never interrupted a conversation.

As I turned into the hotel parking lot, I finally determined that it was all a win. The old Natasha would have sat at a table alone squirming in her seat until Sue was ready to leave.

The next morning Sue waited for me in the lobby to take her to the conference. Social anxiety holds grudges. Social anxiety easily feels abandoned and has an elephant-level memory.

But Paro no longer called the shots. I greeted Sue with a warm smile, and we headed to the parking lot. "Did you have fun last night?" I made sure not to apologize for leaving early. Over-apologizing was a Paro sidekick that I now refused to feed.

"Yes, too much probably. I'm exhausted," she said as she got into the passenger side of my rental car.

The second day was easier than the first. I sat next to Sue, but I no longer cared if she talked to me or not. When you do hard things you adapt quickly. There is only so much you can take before you become comfortable in the discomfort. I guess that was the whole purpose of taking these challenges.

That evening, Sue and I went out for dinner again. The conversation easily flowed, and I was relieved that there were no parties or social gatherings that evening to threaten my calm.

Driving Sue around became routine for the next few days and by the end of the training I felt that I knew her life story. After the training was over, I sat in the airport and reviewed the experience like a seasoned football player would review the play-offs. I watched the replay in my mind's eye, going over conversations and decisions I made during the long weekend. I had done hard things and had come out unscathed. It wasn't fun, but that wasn't the point.

A few days later I got out the business card Sue gave me and found her email address. I was notorious for never following up with new friendships or connections. I emailed her and told her it was nice getting to know her and that I would love to keep in touch. She never responded.

That's okay. I no longer needed outward approval to feel whole. I was getting better.

Chapter 21
Now

I straightened up the fidget toys on my coffee table and lit a candle. I had a full schedule of sessions, but first I needed to close the chapter I had opened with one final meeting.

A part of me was sad that this routine was ending. I had finally caught up with myself. After this session, I had nothing new to offer. I was going to have to fly solo, touching base with myself along the way. Perhaps that doesn't have to be a sad thing, and maybe that's something we should all be doing anyway? Maybe that's what other emotionally healthy people do?

I popped my head out of my office and motioned for Ms. 43 to come in. She was only three years older than the last Natasha, but we had a lot more to cover. She was about to go down a rollercoaster ride she didn't know she was on.

"Well, hello there. We meet again," I said, smirking and motioning her to come in. This was her office as much as it was mine, and I could tell it felt weird for her to sit on the opposite side of the couch and be the identified "patient."

"I know it hasn't been too long since we talked, but a lot is about to change, so I thought it would be good to have one final check-in," I explained.

Her relaxed posture stiffened at the mention of change. I knew she didn't like that word. Change was scary. It meant the unknown and like many other anxious people, she didn't like things she couldn't plot and plan for ahead of time.

"Ooh, I don't like the sound of that," she said, leaning closer, wringing her hands.

I put my hands up, "Nothing bad, I promise. But you are going to grow even more than you have already." I smiled to offer her reassurance and calm her nerves.

"Well, I feel that I've already grown quite a bit," she shrugged. "I have no idea how I can grow anymore."

"We never do until it happens," I explained. "So, let's catch up on what's been going on in the last three years. How are you holding up?"

"Life is good. Chloe is eleven, Xander is five and Alex is three. We moved into a beautiful home we had built. Chloe goes to school in the neighborhood. Xander and Alex still go to that Montessori school that is a little utopia in the desert. Jimmie is closer to his work. It's all good," she said.

"I mean, how are *you* doing?" I reiterated.

She shifted in her seat, looking uncomfortable. "Oh, me? I'm good too. I don't have to work as much. My hours are decent. I can't complain."

I went right in for the kill. "How's it going *socially*?" I already knew the answer.

"Well, it is what it is. I've resigned myself to the fact that I don't think I even want friends. And that's fine. I'm an introvert, so I think I like the *idea* of friends more than the reality of it." She stared off, averting my gaze because she knew I could see past the bullshit she was trying to sell me.

"No new friends in the neighborhood or at the kids' schools?" I prodded, purposely pushing her out of her comfort zone.

"No." She put her hands up in what seemed like defeat. "I'll admit, it was really crushing at first. I had this vision of having a best friend on my block. Someone I could have coffee with and confide in. Someone I could put on my kids' emergency contact forms. God, those forms make me squirm. They make me realize how alone I truly am."

I nodded in agreement, "I know."

"But I'm resigned to the fact that I'm not going to have friends and honestly, it's okay. I don't have time for that anyway."

I leaned forward in my seat. "The goal isn't for you to create this huge social life, that's not who you are. The goal is for you to feel okay with who you are."

She shrugged and shook her head, "Honestly, I just don't know how to do that. I don't even know if that's possible at this point."

I smiled a knowing smile. "It is and it will be, but it will take work. Work that you'll have to keep up for the rest of your life."

She moaned, "That sounds exhausting. I think I'd rather just keep the status quo."

I raised my eyebrows. "You might not have a choice in the next few years. You are about to jump off a social anxiety cliff."

There was new urgency to her voice. "What do you mean by that?"

"I'm just saying that you are going to put yourself out there, more than you ever have before. When we put ourselves front and center, we are more vulnerable for criticism and judgment. You are going to need to grow thicker skin to survive that."

Worried wrinkles forming on her forehead, she said, "Why on earth would I do that? That sounds like creating my own hell on earth. I can't imagine that's something I would wish on myself."

I laughed out loud. "Well, you kind of go into it blindly, but trust me, you don't regret it. It takes you to the next level of acceptance. It was that or drown," I said.

The worried expression remained painted on her face. "You have officially scared me."

"Trust me, this will be nothing compared to what is coming five years later in 2020," I said.

We wrapped up our session and I gave her a tight hug. "I've really enjoyed meeting with each one of you," I said as my eyes watered up. "I'm sad to see this end."

Ms. 43 didn't seem to know what to say. "Thanks," she mumbled. "But any hints for 2020? You're actually making me nervous."

"I wouldn't even know where to begin," I said. "Travel. Soak up the world. Go on a cruise. Stock up on toilet paper," I laughed.

"Um, okay. Totally not helping, but okay," she said, scanning my face to see if I was being sarcastic.

"You'll be fine," I said, opening the door leading to the stairs of the parking lot. As she was heading for her car, I shouted down to her, "I love you!"

She looked up, seemingly touched by the words. "I love you too," she said with a warm smile. "I love you too," she repeated.

Chapter 22
Now

"Hey, how have you been?" It was my youngest sister, Allison. Our conversations had been less and less frequent over the years.

My oldest sister Leigh had joked, "Since your confidence and social anxiety have improved, I don't hear from you anymore." She was joking, but not really. I wondered why that was? She was right, I didn't reach out or call my siblings.

I thought back to the last 20 years or so. I desperately craved the love and feeling of belonging with all my siblings. I jumped up to answer the phone if they called. I traveled across the country if they even slightly hinted that they wanted to see me. Jimmie used to joke that he was jealous of my puppy dog behavior around my brother.

I told myself that our lack of closeness was due to the stress of my mentally ill father or the dysfunction of our childhood. I believed them when they said we were both to blame because I didn't reach out either. I made excuses for them when I wasn't notified about big life events, like when my sister's youngest child was born or when my brother quietly got remarried and I accidentally discovered it on Facebook.

I had voiced my complaints to my mom when she was alive, but she swiftly placed blame directly in my lap, as she often did. "You don't reach out enough. Maybe if you made more of an effort?" I was gaslighted in all directions until the fog of social anxiety lifted and I saw the stark truth. My desperate thirst for belonging had been quenched by my own tall glass of self-acceptance. I was no longer the same person who begged for their attention and belonging.

I had let go of all that hurt and anger that had festered inside me for so long. I had let go of the desire to fix the irreparable. I had become a staunch defender of what I deserved. I had become protective of the little me inside. The young girl who had to walk twice as fast to keep up with her brother. The young girl who hid her tears because she was not allowed to add to the family's chaos. Social anxiety had put me on a hamster wheel of acceptance, and I was ready to get off.

"So, what have you been up to?" Allison asked after there was a lull in conversation. Talking to her had become awkward for me. "Not much. I am working on a new project. I'm writing a memoir on my social anxiety." I just wanted to pull the Band-Aid off.

There was a pause. "Oh wow, that's great." I scanned her words for any hint of annoyance or disappointment. She was the family writer. She had got her master's in fine arts for writing. She had worked at Random House. She was the professional, not me.

"Yeah, it has been really therapeutic," I continued. "It's really helped me get over the whole school bus incident that threw me into such a tailspin."

There was quiet on the other end of the phone. "What bus incident?"

I guess I hadn't told her. She was not the first, second, or even third person I'd reach out to in a crisis. I had told Leigh and getting validation that all those people were crappy had made me feel better, but I guess I didn't talk to Allison. I gave her the short version, still feeling embarrassed by how objectively insignificant the whole thing seemed.

"It wasn't what happened as much as what it brought up for me," I tried to explain, knowing she had no clue about the depths of my social anxiety or maybe about the existence of my social anxiety at all.

"You might want to reconsider traditionally publishing it then," she warned.

My annoyance started to bubble up. "Why?" A flashback of me trying to sell her the virtues of my last self-published book popped into my head.

"Well, if you had that reaction to a post on Facebook, I worry about what your reaction would be to comments or critics of your memoir."

I thought there was irony in her concern. "Well, you know that's kind of the point, isn't it? Wouldn't it be hypocritical if I was writing a book about overcoming social anxiety and I had to self-publish because I was afraid of judgment and criticism? That wouldn't make sense."

I could tell I hadn't made my point. She was out of touch with who I was and who I had become.

* * *

This book sat on the metaphorical shelf collecting dust for a few months after the victories described in the last chapter. My outline was over, and my story had been told. It was time for me to neatly tie this book up in a bow. No words flowed out of me. I found distractions and excuses so I didn't have to come back to it.

How does a book on social anxiety end? With me singing Kumbaya arm in arm with my new group of friends? With me finding my voice and discussing my struggles on a TED Talk stage? I could picture it in my head. "I have dreamed about this moment forever," I would say to the crowd, "and it was one of my worst nightmares." The audience would laugh.

But life doesn't have sharp endings. The sun doesn't set as you walk hand in hand with your happily ever after. I waited for something big and significant to happen in my life so I could wrap up this story with a true Hollywood ending, but it never came.

I sat in a car line waiting to drop my daughter off at school. It was a new school and a new line. I liked this fresh start. I glanced out my window, bored with the wait. I saw a man in a robe walking out of his house. He was staring at the sidewalk so intensely that I shifted my eyes to look at what he was staring at. There was a small pile of poop on the sidewalk. He looked annoyed and briskly walked back into the house.

The line wasn't moving. I crawled half a foot and stopped again.

The man came back out, and I lazily watched him. He

bent over and I imagined he was picking up the poop, but he hovered too long so I squinted to take a closer look. He was steadying his phone. He was taking a picture. He angrily turned around and slammed his door, the poop remaining on the sidewalk.

My imagination took it from there. Him angrily pounding on his keyboard. Him posting the photo as proof of how he was wronged, how the neighborhood was wronged. The dialogue of anger and annoyance would spin up, like a tornado creating chaos on a sunny day. Fingers would be pointed. Maybe it was the quiet girl who walks the black lab or maybe it's the old lady with her poodle. We'll look out our windows tomorrow and see, finger steady, ready to capture it for the world to witness.

The poop was there the next day and the day after that. It was easier to complain than to quietly do something about it.

But this isn't about poop or a school bus. People aren't going to change. We are all at risk of having a bad moment captured for the world to see. We are all at risk of being scrutinized, analyzed, embarrassed, or degraded. That will never change. But how we handle those moments can.

We can choose to give our power away. We can choose to let others define us. We can spend our lives searching for approval, analyzing people's tones and replaying moment after moment, trying to sniff out any signs of rejection.

I had allowed my social anxiety to do just that. I had given Paro the reins and he had happily put me on a rollercoaster of insecurities my entire life. But I have hit the kill switch and that ride has ended. I will no longer allow others to determine my value and worth. I will no longer give my power away. I have taken all my shattered pieces and have glued myself back together. I am not worthy because others tell me so. I am worthy because it is so. I am enough. I have always been enough, I just didn't realize it until now.

I am not naive enough to think that this is how the story ends. To think that I ride off into the empowered sunset feeling confident, never fearing judgment again. I'm human after all. I'll hit bumps and some of them might knock me off my feet, but one thing is for sure, I'll always come up swinging.

Epilogue

Unfortunately, I didn't hit a bump. I hit a boulder, and it crushed everything in its path, leaving complete destruction in its wake.

This book wasn't supposed to have an epilogue. I was supposed to hit a few bumps and be on my way. As close to a Hollywood "Happily Ever After" as I could get in real life.

Now I wonder what I would have told Miss 43. Would I have promised her that everything would be alright? Would I have told her to, "Travel. Soak up the world. Go on a cruise. Stock up on toilet paper" in 2020? Probably not.

What would I have told Miss 48, the one who wrote this book, so confident she was on solid ground? Would I have told her that she was hanging from a branch and was about to freefall? Would I have told her that she was about to go into such a dark abyss that the light would hurt her eyes?

No. Some things are too painful to warn a soul about.

Seven days after I wrote the final words of this book, my world came crashing down. It was a normal school day. I got the kids ready for school, while Jimmie continued to sleep. Jimmie had injured his Achilles tendon during a work training a couple of weeks earlier and had to have outpatient surgery to repair it. It had been a bumpy recovery. He had been sore, fatigued and in pain. I quietly got out of bed to let him sleep in.

After dropping the kids off I decided to run to the grocery store, grab a few items, and get us both a Starbucks. As I came home the house was still quiet. I grew annoyed that he wasn't trying to move around, something he needed to do if he wanted to start recovering. I put his Starbucks green tea in the fridge and went to check on him.

I quietly cracked open the bedroom door. He was still sleeping. I watched for his breathing, a habit I'd had since I was little. I started to close the door when something caught my eye. The blanket was slightly pulled away and his shirt was partially lifted. Adrenaline shot through my body before my brain could register why. Purple blotches spotted his abdomen.

I ran to him and tried to wake him up. I grabbed his face with both my hands and that is when I saw the deep purple spots covering the side of his neck. His usual, overly warm body was cold and unresponsive.

What happened next was a whirlwind of panic and overwhelm. I called 911. I hyperventilated as I tried to explain what was happening. The operator insisted I get him off the bed and on to the floor to do CPR.

"I can't!" I screamed. "He's way too big." I tried to lift his body, but he was twice as big as me.

The operator seemed annoyed, "Can't you get someone to help you? A neighbor or someone?"

"I have no one!" I screamed into the phone. "NO ONE!"

I sobbed, the larger realization sinking in even in the midst of the chaos. My mind flashed to Chloe, upstairs doing online school. I didn't want her to see this scene. It would be permanently, indelibly etched into her mind's eye. There are some things you can never unsee.

I grabbed him once again and strained to lift him up, dragging his body on to the floor. The nightstand with his water and pills from surgery, came crashing to the floor. I started to do CPR until I finally heard the fire department coming through the garage. Time froze as they worked on him for what seemed like forever. Chloe eventually came down and I shielded her from the scene, but she insisted on coming to the hospital.

We were still in the middle of the Covid-19 crisis and the hospital security guard wasn't going to let us into the ER, but for some reason he changed his mind and escorted us to a small room a few feet from where they worked on Jimmie. I knew in my heart that he was already gone, that he had already been gone when I found him. They swarmed around his body. A nurse noticed us staring through an open curtain and quickly shut it. I felt as if I was in a scene from *Grey's Anatomy*. Was this even real?

A few minutes later another nurse came in. "I'm sorry, he's not going to make it," she said softly. "The doctor wants you to come in and be with him for his last moments. We also want you to see that we went above and beyond to try and save him."

I sat in the sterile room where an ER doctor and a team of nurses all dressed in full hazmat suits went through the motions of trying to bring life back to my dead husband.

A machine moved up and down on his chest as they pumped chemicals into him, periodically pausing to see if he had a pulse.

I sat in a chair next to him, holding his cold, limp hand, blood dripping down from a rushed IV. Tears rolling down my face, I wailed through my mask, "Come back. Come back. Come back," over and over again. My mind's eye could see him hovering in the corner of the ceiling watching the chaos unfold. I looked up, pleading with him to return to his body.

I knew he was gone before the ER doctor officially called it. I knew he was gone the minute I saw those purple splotches and felt the coldness of his touch. The one person who kept me safe, who anchored me through all my anxiety, who told me to stop waiting for the other shoe to drop, was now gone.

I felt more alone than I had ever felt in my entire life. I felt angry that he was robbed of a beautiful life, that he left our world with his life only half lived. Jimmie deserved a better ending. He deserved to grow old, get gray hair and hold his grandchildren.

Jimmie was my buffer. He was the fine shell around my fragility. He kept me whole, even through our own relationship struggles. With him gone, I was completely cracked open, my fears and insecurities splattered everywhere. Grief tore through my world and destroyed my foundation.

I felt abandoned and rejected even though I knew it wasn't rational. Even after I read the autopsy report and knew it had been a blood clot from his surgery, I felt as if his soul decided to leave me. I felt as if I wasn't good enough. I played and replayed our story, analyzing it from every angle.

Jimmie always thought he'd die young. His dad died young.

His dad's dad died young. It felt like a curse. We often talked about death. I told him that even though I knew it was selfish, I hoped that I'd die first. I didn't think I would be able to survive without him.

He told me if he were to die the FBI family would swoop into our life and surround us with love and support. "They'll have your back, Natasha. I promise. You won't have to do it alone." I rolled my eyes. He said that often, but I didn't believe him. His look became more serious. "I mean it. I know they'll take care of you if something happens to me." I hated it when he talked like that. I didn't want to imagine it.

Ever since I'd met him I had a reoccurring dream that I was lost in a place I didn't recognize, and I couldn't find my way back to him. I would toss and turn, searching for him all night. In the morning, I would vent about these bad dreams. "It seems that no matter what I dream, it always turns into a bad dream about me being lost, unable to find you."

He would respond, "Better to have bad dreams and a great life, than great dreams and a bad life." He was right. After he died I never had those reoccurring dreams again. I didn't need to, I was now living them.

As he predicted, the FBI swooped in and took care of us. I was handheld through the funeral and burial process. I was escorted to do all the hard things, like planning his service and filling out bureaucratic paperwork. Our doorbell was constantly ringing as strangers showed up or sent gifts in the mail. The kids took a month off school. I permanently closed my therapy practice and took three months off my online work. I felt like a zombie pretending to be alive.

The neighborhood that had caused so much of my social anxiety was now kind. One family showed up repeatedly and brought gifts for my kids. Some people from the community checked in and dropped off gift cards.

Jimmie's sister flew in and helped me with the kids during the first week. My siblings rallied around to support me. Sibling Zoom calls became a staple every Friday and our relationship was rejuvenated. The world didn't look so black and white anymore. There were shades of gray. People weren't all good or all bad. We were all human, doing our human things.

I was forced to do things by myself. I could no longer depend on Jimmie to do things with me or *for* me. My family was spread across the country. I had no friends on speed dial. I had no true friends at all. I started going back to therapy to help me digest my new upside-down world and my place in it.

Initially, the outpouring of support from the FBI, the neighborhood and family members filled the empty void. I was overwhelmed and overloaded with conversations, interactions and pleasantries, but it was a buffer from the inevitable silence that would follow. I was filled with gratitude but uncomfortable with all the help. I wasn't one to ask for help and the attention made me feel weak, like a victim. I was the helper, the one to dole out the support. I didn't like being on the receiving end.

The internet buzzed with my absence. My loss spread from one post to another. I could no longer hide behind the keyboard. His death was very public, and it needed to be. I needed the help from online friends to keep my business afloat.

I needed parents to understand why I had disappeared and be reassured I'd eventually return, that I hadn't abandoned them the way I felt abandoned.

At first I wanted to hide under my blankets. I wanted to shut out the world and live in a remote cabin. I wanted to disappear. I wanted to die.

I seriously contemplated my options. I thought of all the ways I could kill myself and how it would play out afterwards. But each scenario ended with my children having to deal with another loss. I couldn't do that to them, even if it meant I had to live with unrelenting pain.

I wasn't only grieving the loss of my partner and my best friend, I was grieving the loss of our parental and life partnership, I was grieving the loss of the roles we shared. It was like waking up to a world that didn't look quite right.

I had lost my life and no matter how hard I searched, it was gone. All of my routines included him. There were no more Sunday morning breakfasts at Panera together. There was no more division of responsibilities. There were no more retirement plans to travel and grow old together. I had gone to bed with my world intact and woken up with it shattered into a million pieces.

I also had new titles that I despised, like widow and single mom. How could I go to bed married and wake up single? The world no longer made sense to me.

I had my breaking points. Like the time the neighbor messaged me at 10 p.m., a month after Jimmie had died. Her husband noticed that water from our yard was flooding the street.

Sheer panic shot through every bone in my body. This was a Jimmie problem, only Jimmie was no longer here.

I remember standing in that dark street, water gushing into the road, overwhelmed, not knowing what to do or how to do it. My only solution was to text the neighbor back and ask for more help. It wasn't in my DNA to ask for help, but I no longer cared. I no longer cared about anything.

There were new, basic worries, such as who would kill the scorpions in our house? Who would change the water filter, the air filters, the fire alarm batteries? Who would navigate our trips and tell us where we parked?

Throughout my journey with social anxiety, I was able to let go of the need to let others fill the void inside me. I was able to untether those strings and fly on my own. But I always had Jimmie to fill in the gaps, to make me feel complete, my secret hose to fill up my empty well, the cement that oozed into all my broken cracks.

When Jimmie died, I had no one to fill my void. I felt disoriented and fearful. I was incomplete and had no one to complete me. All the energy I had spent chasing his love and approval, sat untapped and unused. At first, I feverishly made a spreadsheet of all the acquaintances I knew and vowed to build up quality friendships. I would make a mental note of who and when I should text to keep the connections going. But this quickly exhausted me.

I was trying to find my new go-to person. I was trying to find a new "Jimmie" to validate me, tell me they'd be there for me, and let me know I was not alone. But I had come too far to go backwards. I needed to learn how to fill my own void.

I needed to find my own completeness. If I did, all my relationships moving forward would be out of love and connection, not based on need and fear.

How many of us have relationships based on our own emptiness? Our own survival instinct to be loved and worthy? What would happen if that love was removed, lost or taken away?

I lost who I was. I didn't know how to be without Jimmie. He was the glue to my self-esteem. He was the cement to my foundation. Without him the ground beneath me was gone and I was freefalling. At first, I felt naked and exposed with no one to shield me from the harshness of life. Like a deer caught alone during hunting season, I felt vulnerable and scared.

No longer did I worry if other people liked me. I had new worries to weigh me down. Who would watch my kids if something happened to me? Would the police even know to check on them if I never returned home?

I had lost everything. My best friend, my confidant, my therapist, my rock, my stability. I was swallowed up whole and consumed by these worries in the beginning. I stopped eating, because everything tasted like cardboard. I stopped sleeping, because my mind was on a perpetual traumatized loop. I felt like a ghost in human clothing. I was barely alive.

I had a morning where I went off the hinges. I threw dishes and had a complete breakdown. As I drove the kids to school the usual entrance was blocked and that's when the tires fell completely off. I cried and screamed and told my kids that I couldn't do this anymore. I had cracked wide open, and I was scaring all of us.

Grief was eating me whole, but the fear of being alone was

devouring me head first. I knew something needed to change. Instead of looking outward, I needed to look inward. No one was going to rescue me, I had to rescue myself.

I had spent most of my life avoiding being alone. Over the last few years, I ventured out to do difficult things alone, but I always returned to the safety and comfort of Jimmie. I was now flying solo and there was no safety net underneath. Both of my parents were dead, and my siblings lived thousands of miles away. I had to depend on myself. This wasn't a challenge on a list I could mark off. This was now my life.

The nights were quiet, empty and excruciating. I learned how to do basic things for myself. I cursed and screamed my way through fitting the right filters into the fridge and the air conditioning. I learned how to replace fire alarm batteries in the middle of the night. I replaced the oven light despite getting an electric shock for the first time. I killed my first scorpion. I replaced our heavy ladder with one I could carry around.

But that was the easy stuff. Jimmie and I did everything together. We showered, grocery shopped and ran errands together. No space in my life existed without him. The only time we were apart was when we were at work. With no social life between us, we were our everything and that had caused its own level of insecurity between us, but that's another story.

I had to learn to be alone, truly alone. It's a process I'm still learning. I cry every day. I sit in silence and listen to my thoughts, to the sounds of nature, to the whispers of grief. I'm getting used to being alone. I am learning how to feel naked in a crowd and be okay. I grocery shop, shower and go to sleep on my own. I take long walks by myself. I take my kids on trips and adventures alone.

Life didn't just knock me off my feet, it catapulted me across the room. It wounded me and left permanent scars. My grief continues to drown me at times, the waves frequently catch me off guard and pull me under. There is a hole in my center that I know will never be filled. I talk to myself. I cry, laugh and hold myself. I check in with myself. All the many versions of me have rallied around, lifting me up, lifting us up, keeping our head just above water, trying to keep us steadily afloat.

Resources

Online course: How to Crush Social Anxiety
https://atparentingsurvivalschool.com/p/crush-social-anxiety
Natasha Daniels walks you through the steps to crush your social anxiety in this on-demand video course.

Follow Natasha Daniels on Instagram and Facebook
@Socialanxietyreality

Visit the author's website
www.socialanxietyreality.com.

National Social Anxiety Center
https://nationalsocialanxietycenter.com
Provides resources and support for social anxiety.

Social Anxiety Institute
https://socialanxietyinstitute.org
Supports groups and provides treatment and resources for social anxiety.

Acknowledgments

To Chloe, Xander and Alex, this book couldn't have been written without you. From squeamish birthday parties to school functions, I was given ample opportunities to face my fears head on. You make me aspire to do better, be better. It is an honor to be your teacher through life and through your own intimate relationships with anxiety. When your dad died, so did our laughter. I've been awed by your resilience and ability to carry the heaviness of grief. You have become my world travelers as we take on new adventures in a life we no longer take for granted.

To Jimmie, I always took life and myself too seriously. It wasn't until I met you that I found the humor in the unfunny, the laughter in the serious. You made me see life from a different perspective. I don't think I ever laughed as much as I did in our 13 years together. I may not have your physical support, but I carry you in my mind and heart. I can hear you crack jokes at all the worst times. I can hear you whisper to me at night to let it all go.

To my siblings, thank you for being willing to read early copies of the book. I know going down memory lane isn't always the most pleasant experience. Your support of this memoir meant the world to me. Also, I will always appreciate how you rallied around me after Jimmie died. Life brings many chapters and I never thought we'd all be as close as we are today. I guess Mom was right when she used to tell us we'd always have each other.

Jimmie's death made me realize that social anxiety was robbing me of deep, meaningful friendships. I have been fortunate to have several friendships develop since then. To Patricia, you have always been a cheerleader for all I do, even before Jimmie died. I value our conversations and your presence in my life. To Jenny, you are truly a bright light in anyone's darkness. To Andrea, you showed up after Jimmie died and have been a supportive presence ever since. To Nicole, who would have thought that our work acquaintance friendship would turn into this deep connection 20 years later? I love our Sunday breakfasts. To Sandie, who helps shift my perspective and always has wise words to share.

To Amanda Peterson, who has become more than a life coach, but a true anchor in the rough seas of grief, parenting and anything else life wants to throw at me. I'm a better person, parent and human being because of our work together.

To all the kids and families I have worked with along the way, I hope you see yourself in these stories. I hope this book reminds you of the work we did and the strength you have inside you.

To Rachael Herron, your writing classes took this mess of clay and helped me mold it into something I can feel proud of. This book could not have been written without you.

If it were not for Jane Evans and the team at Jessica Kingsley Publishers, this story would be sitting on a shelf collecting dust. Thank you for believing in this story and giving it life. It is always a joy to work with you all.

And to you, the person reading this book, the one who often feels invisible. I hope you felt seen as you read this book. I hope you felt inspired. I know social anxiety can be a lonely experience, but I hope you now know, you are not alone.